THE
MAD
POTTER
OF
BILOXI

GARTH CLARK

ROBERT A. ELLISON, JR.

EUGENE HECHT

PHOTOGRAPHY

BY JOHN WHITE

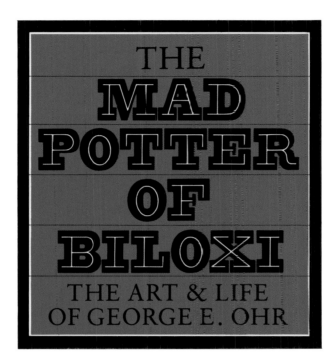

SPECIAL CONSULTANT

MARTIN SHACK

ABBEVILLE PRESS

PUBLISHERS

NEW YORK

LONDON

Editor: Constance Herndon
Copyeditor: Susan Neitlich
Designer: Warren Infield
Copy chief: Robin James
Production supervisor: Hope Koturo

Frontispiece:
Handled, footed vase, c. 1895—1900.
Height: 11¼ inches. Private collection,
New York.

Page 8:
Footed vase, c. 1898—1907.
Height: 5 inches. Private collection,
New York.

Library of Congress Cataloging-in-Publication
Data

Clark, Garth, 1947—
    The mad potter of Biloxi: the art and
    life of George E. Ohr / Garth Clark,
    Robert Ellison, Eugene Hecht.
            p.   cm.
    Photography by John White.
    Bibliography: p.
    Includes index.
    ISBN 0-89659-927-2
    1. Ohr, George E., 1857-1918—
    Criticism and interpretation.
2. Pottery, American—Mississippi—Biloxi. I.
Ellison, Robert. II. Hecht, Eugene. III. White,
John, 1950 Nov. 23- IV. Title.
NK4210.042C5   1989
738′.092—dc20   89-6978
                                          CIP

Contents

Every once in a great while an artist comes along whose work is so wonderful, so imaginative, and yet so close to the nerve that it engages and excites us immediately without our knowing why—the joy of creation is almost palpable and the intellectual labor all-too-often required to appreciate a work of art is rendered happily superfluous. This kind of immediate, raw aesthetic energy is the hallmark of George E. Ohr, America's consummate artist-potter and one of the most fascinating characters ever to spring from the Mississippi mud. During his life (1857–1918) the self-styled Mad Potter of Biloxi was condescendingly dismissed by the era's artists and critics. But this turn-of-the-century master from the backwaters of Mississippi was far from crazy. While the eccentric Ohr still remains relatively unknown, today his genius has finally begun to be recognized. The purpose of our book is to give this radical, sophisticated, and deeply moving artist his due—a purpose we cannot hope to fulfill but one we are proud at least to initiate.

This project was launched in the mid-1980s when Marty Shack encouraged the three of us to join forces and produce a book about Ohr. All of us were ardent followers of the maverick potter and had separately fallen under his spell over a decade earlier. Driven by a contagious delight, we had spent considerable effort researching the extant documents and studying every detail of the work long before we met as a group. The next apostle to join the project was the photographer John White, who had already worked with Ohr's ceramics and whose tremendous skill, enthusiasm, and patience have produced both technically and aesthetically outstanding images. The book that has resulted is a product of our shared conviction that the Mad Potter of Biloxi was indeed an incomparable genius whose art need only be put before the modern world to be appreciated —something that Ohr himself often asserted.

A number of people have given us considerable assistance during the creation of this book and we would like to extend our gratitude to them. First, Marty Shack provided us with invaluable information, documentation, and, on a more personal level, much good-humored support. We would also like to thank the many collectors who allowed us access to their homes and the marvelous pots in their care, and to extend our appreciation to our families and friends who endured the demands and disruptions engendered by the project. Special thanks are offered to Mark Magowan and Sharon Gallagher at Abbeville Press, who believed in the book and helped make it a reality. We are indebted as well to our patient and politic editor, Constance Herndon, and to our imaginative designer, Warren Infield. Thanks are also extended to Dawn Bennett for stepping in with organizational assistance at the eleventh hour, to Mark Del Vecchio for his support and encouragement, to Estelle Shack for her hospitality and support, and to Carolyn Eisen Hecht for the research hours she spent in the archives. Robert A. Ellison, Jr., would also like to express his appreciation to Rosaire Appel and Martin Eidelberg for their invaluable comments on his manuscript. We would also like to thank Alice Cooney Frelinghuysen, Gary and Diana Stradling, Paul Evans, J. W. Carpenter, and Bobby Davidson Smith for sharing their thoughts and knowledge.

As the reader will soon discover, we have not striven for a consensus of opinion in these essays. Ohr left behind little documentation of his sources and inspirations, and only fragments suggesting the chronology of his life, a situation that has engendered a variety of interpretive viewpoints. Until more information is unearthed, the plurality of opinion that characterizes this study seems perfectly appropriate. But this book is only the beginning; in the end, Ohr's work stands magnificently on its own.

G. C.
R.A.E.
E. H.

Part 1: *The Early Years*

T he one-hundredth anniversary of the emergence of American cotton into the world market might seem an unlikely event to celebrate, but in the South, which remained in the shadows of Civil War Reconstruction, there was surely need for celebration. After modest yet creditable exhibitions on that theme in Atlanta (1881) and Louisville (1883), the concept gained country-wide appeal. And so, by act of Congress, in February 1883, the National Cotton Planters' Association was duly empowered to organize a glorious international exposition of art and industry—seventy-six acres under roof. To be sure, a homage to King Cotton should properly rival the great fairs of Philadelphia (1876) and Paris (1878). New Orleans, chief among the cities of the Cotton Belt, was to host this American show of modernity. To underscore the significance of the event, on December 16, 1884, President Chester A. Arthur himself, sitting in the East Room of the White House, telegraphed the signal that officially opened the World's Industrial and Cotton Centennial Exposition.

For the next six months New Orleans literally shone: the fair was ablaze in electric light. Urbane and cosmopolitan, at least temporarily, it bustled with celebrities, dignitaries, and intellectuals, with foreign craftsmen and Northern entrepreneurs, with exotic strangers in caftan and kimono. Every kind of wonder was there in the little displays and pavilions. Visitors gawked at mounds of Mexican silver and mused on the lifelike dummy of a Chinese merchant surrounded by his wares. They petted pigs and strolled through a hut made of sugarcane and rice stalks. They watched the machines endlessly turning out barbed wire; there were gins and engines, generators and lathes, thread-spinning machines and wood-working machines—machinery everywhere.

There too, ensconced among the multitude, absorbed in the whir of his little handmade potter's wheel, was an extraordinary young man on his way to becoming an even more extraordinary artist. George E. Ohr (1857–1918), a person of intense individuality and creative passion, was America's archetypal artist-potter, though only he could have known it then. These months on the fairground, competing for attention with the barbed-wire machine and the prized pigs, were early in his newfound career and quite an education. No doubt he spent long hours, much as he would in years to come, as a petty showman, though surely in virtuoso performance, magically whirling clay into familiar forms, dissolving one into the next for the entertainment of the passersby, who might even be moved to purchase a trinket or two. In 1885 George Ohr was a country boy in the big city with no reputation and less money, having spent a year's savings just getting his wares to the exposition. Little is known of that work other than that it was true to his already abiding commitment to individuality: he had put out a display of "over 600 pieces, no two alike."[1]

Ohr was born on Sunday, "10 A.M. sharp," the 12th of July, 1857, in Biloxi, Mississippi, to Johanna (Wiedman[2]) and George Ohr. A few months later he was christened George Edgar in the Episcopal Church of the Redeemer. Johanna had come to the South from Württemberg, Germany, and met George, *der alter,* an Alsatian blacksmith, in New Orleans in 1853. They soon married and set up house in the little Gulf-port town, where they established the first smithy in Biloxi. Later when the railroad came through Harrison County, they opened the first grocery store, over on the corner of Pass Christian Street (now Howard Avenue) and Delauney.

George E. was the second of five children and always saw himself as the family misfit—"3 hens, 1 rooster and a duck." He was that defiant duck, picked on and punished, forever in "hot aqua," and yet strangely pleased with the role. Young George attended elementary school in Biloxi for a while and went to "German school" in New Orleans one winter, but that was the extent of his formal education. The next winter he apprenticed to a file cutter and then some time later to a tinker. He apparently learned the blacksmith's trade at his father's shop, but the two don't seem to have gotten along at all well. In his midteens, having already become familiar with hard labor, George lit out on his

The Times
and
Life of
G. E. Ohr

BY EUGENE HECHT

Figure 1
Joseph Meyer and George Ohr possibly at Newcomb College, probably in the late 1880s.

own for New Orleans, Louisiana. Over the next two years or so, he worked fifteen hours a day in the warehouse of a ship's chandler. Finally saying goodbye to the "old boss sponge" who ran the supply store, George signed aboard a sailing ship. "But the sea had no charms for him, and after one voyage, he was glad to return to Biloxi and to his father."[3]

Back home in Mississippi the young roustabout held a number of odd jobs, content with none of them. Then came a turning. Sometime around 1879 Ohr received a letter from Joseph Fortune Meyer (1848–1931), a boyhood friend. That timely missive was an invitation to come to New Orleans, learn the potter's trade, and make a respectable ten dollars a month while doing it. Ohr jumped at the offer. Meyer was a fellow Alsatian who had learned the craft from his father, François Antoine. At one time the elder Meyer had a pottery on Back Bay in Biloxi. The family then moved to New Orleans where François opened a shop, making and selling utilitarian crockery in the old French market in the Vieux Carré.[4] Before he died François also started a little boot and shoe store on Saint Bernard Avenue, and for the next two decades son Joseph alternated between pottery and dry goods depending on the exigencies of life.[5,6]

Young George, delighted with the notion of flying off to New Orleans to see an old friend, packed his bag and stole aboard a freight, traveling the eighty miles along the Gulf coast compliments of the Louisville & Nashville Railroad. He took rooms at 406 Delord and promptly began his apprenticeship. Meyer was an established person, a fine, traditional potter interested in turning out solid, attractive, practical ware. "There was a spice to his conversation peculiarly wise and shrewd. Voltaire could not have been more caustic; . . . living almost to the condition of penury, yet withal a most delightful host."[7] The two got along marvelously. Joseph was nine years Ohr's senior and a natural role model; kind and patient, he was a man who loved his craft and was willing to share its valued secrets. The whole experience was a revelation to George: "When I found the potter's wheel I felt it all over like a wild duck in water."[8] Ohr had discovered his special gift of hand and mind and now slowly, haltingly, in the beginning

even unknowingly, he would evolve an intensely personal human vision that would give his work the profundity of all great art.

And there he was in New Orleans, peacock-pleased with himself, good-looking, sporting a thick, well trimmed moustache and a jaunty cap (to keep the clay dust out of his dark hair). Sleeves rolled to the elbow and clad in a proper long workman's apron—the canvas kind that carries its own sense of purpose—Ohr at the tender age of about twenty-two had found himself (Figure 1). He was a potter, and not ashamed to tell the world.[9] He would spend the rest of his days redefining the meaning of the word *potter,* and in so doing, refining the very meaning of his life.

With a penchant for independence and a flowering egocentricity, journeyman George, from the start, probably designated the pieces he made with some sort of mark of his own. Always the native son, it's not surprising to find *Biloxi* scrawled or impressed on his earliest work. Indeed, among country potters, and George at the time was a country potter, it was common to use ordinary printer's letters to impress a logotype into the soft clay—a practice George kept to, with some variation, for almost twenty years.[10]

Youthful and impatient, Ohr resettled himself in quarters on Euphrosine Street but that wasn't nearly enough of a change to satisfy his wanderlust: "After knowing how to boss a little piece of clay into a gallon jug I pulled out of New Orleans and took a zigzag trip for 2 years, and got as far as Dubuque, Milwaukee, Albany, down the Hudson, and zigzag back home. I sized up every potter and pottery in 16 States, and never missed a show window, illustration or literary dab on ceramics since that time, 1881."[11] Gone for much of 1881 and 1882, he returned to New Orleans and took a job at the William Virgin Pottery. He also probably did some work for Meyer, who was still potting during those years (though by 1884 Joseph would be running a "variety store," selling boots and shoes for the next five years). George worked in the city until the latter part of 1883 when he returned home (most likely motivated by the closing of Meyer's pottery). In any event,

Figure 2
G. E. Ohr posing in a photography
studio in Biloxi, c. 1892.

off to Biloxi he went, a total savings of $26.80 in his pocket, twenty-six years old, a traveler and a potter, determined to make his own way.

Not being able to afford either room or board, Ohr moved back into his parental home and soon began spending what he did have—time in abundance—building his pottery. Already a retired blacksmith, George E. was himself able to fabricate all the ironwork (the strapping for the wood-burning kiln, the grinding teeth for the clay mill). Everything he made by hand; even the potter's wheel, and that exchange of sweat and skill for the tools of the trade was both an economic necessity and a physical expression of the philosophy of his life's work. His cash went mostly for kiln bricks "and like the mud wasp," he tells us, he made his kiln "with lime, then with grit and credit." When some pine trees came into his possession, he had them sawed into boards, then rafted the lumber downriver and hauled it to the site by himself. Working totally alone he constructed his first small shop.[12] To stretch his meager resources as far as possible, he swiped as many

supplies as he could, most of them probably from his father's shop, and "the old man kicked like a circus mule . . . but momma said: Let the boy go on, and watch him."[13]

In those early days he got his clay free for the digging (as Meyer had) from the banks of the nearby Tchoutacabouffa River. George would row a barge out to the place where the mud was good, work for hours loading up, and then row back on the next high tide. Docked on Back Bay, he struggled to haul home the great load of wet, raw clay. The Blacksmith Potter, as he came to be called, knew all about the commercial imperatives of survival; he spent much of his time making flue pipes and water jars, flower pots, planters, and pitchers. These humble earthenware goods he peddled door to door from a hand-built pushcart. That was his first year in business (1883 to 1884), and the housewives of Biloxi gave him a modest profit for his efforts. In all it was a particularly exciting time; everyone was talking about and preparing for the upcoming world's fair in New Orleans—George too had his plans. With a selection of some six hundred pieces of his ware, spending almost all his year's savings on portage alone, G. E. Ohr went off to the Cotton Centennial Exposition to show the whole world his stuff.

The well-known suffragette Julia Ward Howe (of "Battle Hymn of the Republic" fame) was the director of the Woman's Department of what was then popularly called the New Orleans Exposition. She arranged to borrow the services of William Woodward, an art professor newly arrived at Tulane University. He was to organize arts and crafts courses that would be given on the exposition grounds. William, in turn, had his brother Ellsworth join the university faculty and the exposition effort. The latter taught a series of highly successful classes to crowds of eager women who came daily to the fair.

As the spring of 1885 slowly dissolved in the warmth of Louisiana June, so too did the World's Industrial and Cotton Centennial Exposition. The wetlands surrounding New Orleans blanketed it in a humidity that became enervating during the long summer from June to October.

Figure 3
Ohr turning out a large pot at the New Orleans Art Pottery, 1889, in a drawing by Professor William Woodward. Joseph Meyer is working in the background on the left. Louisiana State Museum, New Orleans.

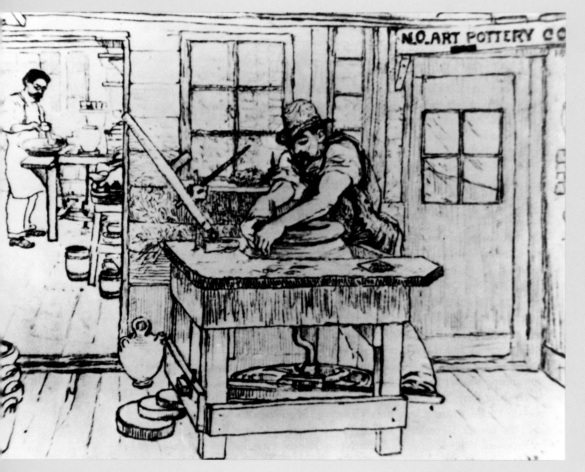

It didn't make much difference that great pumps flushed the open gutters in all the streets daily when the weather turned hot. No one of any means would stay in the city then, not into the "sickly season" with the yellow fever still so virulent. The closing days of the fair were met with mixed emotions, but for Ohr, who was still rather naive, it brought a personal disaster: he had packed his belongings, "ware, stand and fixings," and arranged to have someone cart them away, and away they went, all of his treasure, everything stolen.[14]

In the fall of 1885, as if to continue their work of the exposition, the Woodward brothers organized free classes on campus under the auspices of Tulane University. Among the offerings were courses in the decorative arts for women two nights a week. Out of that venture arose an organization called the Ladies' Decorative Art League, which, in conjunction with the university, would develop the needed programs. They rented space for classrooms on Baronne Street, near Delord Street (now Howard Avenue[15]) in New Orleans. Within a year or so (1886) the league took a small, two-story brick building across the street, at what was then 249 Baronne. There they charted and outfitted the New Orleans Art Pottery to service the practical needs of their students for glaze and fire. And who should they hire to tend the kilns and throw the pots the ladies would subsequently decorate, but a well-known dry-goods merchant, one Joseph Fortune Meyer.[16]

In all probability George returned to Biloxi after the fair, but since the freight cars of the Louisville & Nashville Railroad provided him inexpensive transport, there's no telling where he was most of the time. One thing is for sure, he was already romantically involved with a Miss Josephine Gehring, a lovely, blue-eyed New Orleans belle who wasn't even eighteen. She was born in Louisiana (September 25, 1868), and, like George, was of German descent. George and Josie (as he often called her) were married on September 15, 1886, in Biloxi.[17]

The lure of free room and board, with two mouths to feed, would keep Pot-Ohr-E-George at the wheel in Biloxi for a while; besides, Josie was pregnant before the honeymoon was over.

Figure 4
The Biloxi Pottery, c. early 1893, as it appeared in *Harper's Magazine*, May 1895.

The younger Ohrs moved in with the older Ohrs in the little house at 409 Delauney and Josie proved herself a lifelong, hardworking provider of strength and support for the ever-growing assembly. Little Ella Louisa was born on the twenty-first of June, 1887, but sadly, she passed away only months later (December 1887).[18]

Now a serious family man, George must have done tolerably well over the next several years, well enough at least to be motivated to construct a new workshop in 1888—put up on his father's land. It was a two-story frame building with a tall peaked roof, not very grand but a sizeable structure by Biloxi standards. At 411 Delauney, it was next door to the house and just behind mother Johanna's grocery, right off Pass Christian Street. Running parallel to the road, the pottery's long portico-like ledge served as a shelf for displaying wares, especially the larger garden planters that wouldn't sit well high on the roof edge (Figure 4). "The Gulf coast has only two cold spells in each winter—

one in November and one in February. When these come they are found to bring a temperature like that of boarding-house tea."[19] So George didn't bother putting glass in the windows—if a storm blew up he could always close the shutters.

By the spring of 1888 Josie was pregnant again and the little shop, too, was beginning to bulge with fresh fictile ware. Asa Eugene, their first son, was born in January of 1889; alas, he too would pass away as a child, weeks before his fifth birthday (in December 1893).[20] The loss of two innocent babes touched George deeply, and the poignant analogy between the glorious Creator and His clay, and the humble creator and his clay, was never far from his mind. It is not insignificant that this sensitive, complex genius came to call his artistic creations "mud babies" and that he could never bring himself to part with them even when they were inadvertently broken or destroyed.

It was probably in 1888 when the self-proclaimed Biloxi Mud Dauber received yet another offer from Joseph Meyer, this one to come and assist him in his work for the Ladies' League. In addition to any other inducements, not the least of which would be a regular salary, the anticipation of showing off his prodigious skills on the wheel to the young women of New Orleans would not have been unappealing to George. He was a rather picaresque fellow, ribald and quite improper—after all, he had hung around with sailors and even been one as a youth. So George packed his bag one more time. The city directory for 1889 carries the entry: "Ohr George E potter, r. 249 Baronne." He had indeed joined "Uncle Joe" Meyer at the New Orleans Art Pottery.

There he worked hunched over the wheel, pumping its treadle, whirling all sorts of ware, and taking particular delight in forming huge garden pots and jardinieres. Shirt sleeves rolled up high enough to reveal his massive biceps, George, always the showman, threw those gigantic pots with uncanny ease. The ever-present apron and some sort of hat (into which he tucked his long hair) completed the uniform. He was now thirty-one years old, vigorous and strong, "a man of dark complexion, with dark

piercing eyes,"[21] not very tall and really slight of build, except for those powerful blacksmith's arms. A dark moustache and beard, already grown full and fairly long, accented his wild eyes and made memorable his handsome face.

Several pieces of pottery from this era exist today and there are pictures of still others.[22,23] They are all in Meyer's restrained, traditional aesthetic: there is no hint here of Ohr's unrivaled virtuosity, of his mastery of the delicate, of his gift for creating tension and rhythm in the clay itself. A few of these pieces are adorned with rather amateurish winged dragons in a grotesque variation on an oriental theme. But even that sculptural motif was not a new one; Maria Longworth Nichols, the founder of the famous Rookwood Pottery, had already passed through her ugly-Japanese-dragon period.[24] Anyone with the price of a *Harper's Magazine*[25] could study that standard of the decorative arts as set forth by the esteemed lady from Cincinnati. These rather self-important New Orleans dragons were not-quite-avant-garde handiwork of students, neither surprising nor skillful.

Newcomb College, the women's division of Tulane, opened its doors in September of 1887 just a few blocks away from the Ladies' Decorative Art League, and the Woodward brothers were charged with organizing its fledgling art department. As the department flourished, students transferred to it and the League gradually lost its *raison d'être*. Even as Ohr and Meyer labored at the New Orleans Art Pottery Company, it became increasingly difficult for the Baronne Street venture to succeed as a business. The pottery was actually a corporation, and when in late December of 1889 it finally found itself without adequate operating funds, it did the corporate thing, evaporating along with its liabilities. The remaining physical facilities were forthwith taken over by the newly formed Art League Pottery Club, presided over by Professor William Woodward; that was in the very beginning of 1890. Meyer probably stayed on, but it's very doubtful that Ohr remained in New Orleans much longer.[26]

One can only speculate on the effect that the experience at the New Orleans Art Pottery might have had on Ohr—it was certainly a far

Figure 5
Small redware pitcher, typical of Ohr's early utilitarian ware. Private collection, New York.

more sophisticated and stimulating environment than Biloxi. Here there were all kinds of educated people, indeed professors, seriously involved however ineffectually in the perfection of ceramics as a decorative art form. Furthermore he could watch professional artists, as well as students, drawing and sculpting,[27] and he could see the vessels that he had molded or thrown being carefully decorated. It's remotely possible that Ohr's charming, often sarcastic, little reptiles, which occasionally crawl about on his later work, were in part a response to the clumsy dragons of New Orleans.[28] But just being at an art pottery, even one that never succeeded in creating one memorable piece, must have forced him to confront a range of artistic issues.

Ohr had learned the trade from Meyer, who was then a traditional rural potter, so it's not surprising to find lovely examples of folk holloware among his earliest pieces. As was customary these were decorated by brushing, sponging, dripping, or spattering with glaze colorants; copper oxide greens and manganese dioxide browns were favorites. The young Pot-Ohr was partial to the deep brown that iron oxide created, so rich it thickened into black. The final step was an all-over coat of high-gloss, low-fired transparent glaze that often had a slightly yellowish tinge. Meyer had given his protégé the formulas for his old-country lead glazes: the kind that might begin with a handful of white lead buckshot for the flux, which lowered the fusing temperature, followed by a sprinkling of kaolin to inhibit running, and of course, the main ingredient, finely ground silica, the stuff that melts and fuses into glass. Indeed legend in the post-war South has it that youngsters would make pocket money scouring the battlefields for lead bullets to sell to the local potters.

The little handcrafted redware pitcher in Figure 5 exemplifies the care George invested in his utilitarian pieces and it's a classic example of folk pottery. The body and lid have been decorated by stamping on color with a chunk of sponge to repeat the pattern all around the vessel. The spoon-worn inside and a few rim nicks attest to the service it saw in Mississippi kitchens. Interestingly the end of the handle meets the body in a V-shaped terminus formed by pressing the clay between the thumb and index finger—a tiny detail, yet a lifelong aspect of Ohr's handling of handles.

Working on his own, the Biloxi Mud Dauber gradually and deliberately moved beyond the realm of the folk potter, though he never forgot what he had learned. The tall ewer in Figure 75 is dated June 20, 1891, and on the bottom, inscribed in script, is *G E Ohr—Art Potter*. And just about a year later, there he proudly stands (Figure 2) properly posed behind a homemade sign that boldly proclaims him ART POTTER. To be sure, there is no formal way to distinguish the work of a folk potter from that of an art potter; the distinction is a matter of intention, which may or may not be reflected in the work itself. The art potter (or more generally the artist) has the primary motivation of creating art (whatever that may be) regardless of its utility, while the folk potter (or more generally, the craftsman) seeks to create objects of specific utility, however artful.

Given that art is created with the specific intention of being art, then the New Orleans Art Pottery was an art pottery, just as the little sign proclaiming George's intentions gave birth philosophically to the Biloxi Art Pottery. In the final analysis, however, each creation must

Figure 6
George, Asa, Leo, Josephine, and Clo posing for a family portrait in Biloxi, c. summer 1892.

speak for itself. And the central question becomes, are we emotionally or intellectually touched by it, are we significantly moved *somehow* by simply perceiving it? At the very least we can say that the successful object of art was intended to reach us in some way and that it continues to do so profoundly, though not necessarily in the intended way, nor, indeed, always in the same way. The work must speak for itself if it is to be successful, if it is truly to be art. Moreover it must draw from some basic wellspring of the sustained human condition, or time will turn it trivial.

The faint photo in Figure 2 is a wonderful document of the young art potter and some of his best work of the early 1890s. The shapes are all traditional; the banding, ruffles, scrolls, and well-defined feet are familiar devices— they can each be found, for example, on the late-nineteenth-century folk pottery of the Shenandoah Valley.[29] And yet there are strong suggestions of what's to come, of Ohr's blend of elegance and presence. This is especially true of the dark middle vase (top row), whose crown has a very interesting crinkled configuration. The large thick-walled vase is turned like all the others, but its mid-section was probably pressed against a plaster mold to form the raised repoussé decoration. Its awkward, undersized scroll handles were rolled by hand and affixed to the body later. The two simple-shaped vases (top row on either end) seem to have some sort of modeling around the bases of their cylindrical necks. The one on the right is especially suggestive but the photo is too indistinct to be completely sure—it would seem that the Biloxi reptiles may already have made their appearance. The tall ewer (lower left) was never glazed; its white-bisque body sports a broad (1¼ inches across), hand-fashioned, flamboyant handle in the style of the purely outrageous. By contrast the two middle vases bear the same molded staghorn handles (of which there were several variations). Like the scrolled handle on the large vase, these too are quite impractical; closing in on themselves, they have no opening for the fingers to grip them.

At the time Ohr was also applying molded clusters of rosettes and embossing cherubs in the manner of Victorian porcelains and metal-

work—a touch of the Rococo Revival of the 1850s. The five-foot-tall bisque vase (dated 6–15–92) standing at the corner of the pottery, just behind and visible above and below the carriage in Figure 4, is embellished with all these devices. A scene of youngsters ice skating decorates one side, a couple dancing the other. The complicated handles (which did not survive intact) were bolted to the body. By now a mainstay in the shop were "fac-simile old style pitchers in use 150 years ago." Doubtless the tourists and fair-goers were fond of them; you could engrave your own name into the damp clay along with the date of the visit if you wished as a practical memento. *E. W. Morrill March 9th 1892* is inscribed across the neck of a rugged, green and brown, five-pint pitcher decorated with ivy vines, billowing plumes, and cherubs playing instruments. One of these cherubial medallions is identically repeated on the five-foot vase and must have been formed with the same mold.

And if a pitcher was too large to carry around, the potter had a variety of small trinkets—clay novelties he called them. They were his stock-in-trade, sold at the local country fairs where George performed. Among the popular favorites, the charming ceramic men's hats, three or four inches across, could also be personalized with inscriptions. His set of low-relief molded plaques of famous Southern buildings were the kind of thing the tourists especially liked.[30] Inexpensive children's banks were a popular item with folk potters at the time and Happy George turned them out by the dozen. They were usually made so that the handful of pennies they enveloped could not be got at without literally breaking the bank and having to buy another. To make them throw-away cheap they were fired only once and rarely glazed. Mr. Ohr offered an extensive line of charming little depositories including ones in the shapes of tops, pears, potatoes, plums, plumb bobs, toadstools, and sugar bowls. One carries the inscription *Sweet Olive Merry Xmas 92*, probably scratched into the damp clay with the point of a large safety pin, one of the very few tools he used.[31]

Somewhere along the way he no doubt noticed with amusement how his own mark, GEO. E.

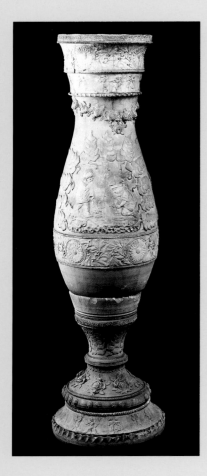

Figure 7
Five-foot-tall bisque vase, dated *6-15-92*, by Ohr (see Plate 26).

OHR, stamped a thousand times on a thousand pots, repeated his given name with his initials. It must have struck him as wonderful because when his second son was born (September 1890) the boy was christened Leo Ernest so that his initials would be L.E.O. By the arrival of the next child, George was quite pleased with the game and no longer felt the need to be even as conservative as he had. Clo Lucinda was born in May of 1892. Ohr's disregard for convention was already a life-style. In July 1893 the *Biloxi Herald* carried the news that "another potter arrived at the art pottery of Geo. Ohr last Wednesday. Of course it was a boy." That little potter was Lio Irwin.

It wasn't long before the Biloxi Art and Novelty Pottery was overflowing, spilling earthenware out into the street. By the spring of 1893 the long portico shelf was heavy with garden urns, water bottles, jardinieres, and pedestals; hanging planters swung in the breeze above them, and a table below was cluttered with coffee pots, vases of all shapes and sizes, a statue of a goat, and a bust on a dark base. Vases and ewers sat on the ground, along with a pretty staghorn-handled piece with folded top, and an ornate window box. Vessels were everywhere— "Rustic, Ornamental, New and Ancient Shaped Vases, Etc."—lined up along the edge of the roof and balanced atop inverted flower pots fitted over the pickets of a fence. Father Geo. E. posed (Figure 8) with his clay babies, between the monumental pink bisque vase with the skaters and a ceramic bottled-water holder (bossed with a molded head at its middle and a frieze of figures around the top), standing just behind Asa and Leo.[32]

Though he worked in the distant isolation of "sleepy old Biloxi" the Unequaled Variety Potter was a serious student of the ancient art. Ever since the Crystal Palace Exposition in London in 1851, international fairs were held in Europe and America at an almost frantic pace, and they became increasingly extravagant. George hadn't made it to Paris in 1889, but the next great fair was to be in Chicago and that was only eight hundred miles away, due north by train. The World's Columbian Exposition held at Jackson Park welcomed the public through its gates on May 1, 1893, though it was

far from complete at that time. For Ohr this was a tremendously important event, bringing together in one place choice examples of artware from all over the world. It was an opportunity to see the latest work of all the famous potteries, an opportunity he couldn't miss.[33] Indeed, the Biloxi Potter set up a display of his wares, probably in the maze of exhibits on the Midway Plaisance, the mile-long strip that came to be called the side show. The great White City, which had opened to cheers and cannon six months before, closed in sad silence on October 30, 1893: the Mayor of Chicago had been assassinated two days before and the people were still grieving. It is not known when George went south, but he was certainly home before Christmas.[34]

The first permanent settlement in the Mississippi Valley, Biloxi had long been a summering place for well-to-do New Orleans folk. The Queen City of the Gulf stretches along the low ridge of a slender east-west peninsula separating the Bay of Biloxi to the north from the Mississippi Sound to the south. Its narrow un-

Figure 8
The Biloxi Art and Novelty Pottery, c. mid-1893—a queer, pink, painted shop, as the *New Orleans Daily Picayune* travel column described it that year.

paved streets, many surfaced white with crushed oyster shells, were bordered in grass and dotted with pretty cottages. Willow, chinaberry, cypress, magnolia, orange, pecan, apple, peach, plum, and of course great live oak trees grew in marvelous abundance. Pass Christian Street

17

Figures 9–11
George was George's most extravagant creation.

(which the locals pronounced *pass chris-CHAN*) was the backbone of the town with its one- and two-story frame business structures. That main thoroughfare ran from the eastern end of the peninsula along its length to Porter Street. North and south from Pass Christian radiated tiny lanes, one of which was Delauney. The pottery was a few hundred feet south, on the west side of that little street, only "3 squares from the L. and N.R.R. depot."

Biloxi (which was Indian for "first people") was already becoming a resort city that made playing, along with fishing, its principal business. Northerners, at first mostly from the West, had already discovered this charming perpetual summerland by the late 1880s. They would come, usually by train, from Michigan, Wisconsin, Iowa, and Illinois, winter over, and then leave in summer when the New Orleans folk returned.

The astute proprietor of the pottery recognized that his clientele could be expanded by tapping into the tourist trade. If he could do that without being distracted from his mission of creating art he might even be able to provide some of the small comforts for his ever-growing family. By nature a high spirited, fun-loving, theatrical character, George found it particularly easy to make a spectacle of himself. He could perform wonders on the wheel, entertain as it were, and sell his wares at the same time. Signs went up everywhere around Biloxi—feisty, provocative, arrogant, grandiose signs luring the tourists to the Pot-Ohr-E. For much of the rest of his life George would be an undignified, irrepressible self-publicist (no doubt following the lead of a less blatant James Whistler). He was so successful at it that by 1894 he had already become an established attraction on the tourist route around the Gulf coast. New Orleans' *Daily Picayune* (October 1894) described the venture as "the famous pottery of Geo. Ohr, whose shop during the past several years has been visited by hundreds of visitors from other sections and from almost every state in the Union seeking relics [souvenirs] in artistic pottery."[35]

As time went on Ohr cultivated his already idiosyncratic persona, becoming increasingly bohemian, increasingly eccentric. The nonconformist instincts of his youth flourished in the drone of the wheel, in the struggle with his art. The imperative to reach beyond boundaries, to travel a singularly innovative course—"no two alike"—carried him and his creations well beyond the ordinary. Great work, great struggle, puts life in its own perspective and smiles knowingly on the bizarre.

The Pot-Ohr "knew how to attract attention, wearing long hair and knotting it on top with a brass pin. His beard similarly of great length was tucked in his shirt front to keep it from the clay as he worked at the wheel. His moustache, was sufficiently long to be placed over his ears."[36] In the end, George was George's most extravagant creation. Besides, eccentricity made good business sense: he was rarely willing to sell any of his artware, yet he had to sell something, why not sell himself? This wasn't some fine shop in New York with chandeliers and carpets, where art was purchased by the cognoscenti. Here a casual vacationer leisurely passing the day could watch a virtuoso performance, get a look at a genuine local oddity—none other than the (almost) legendary Mad Potter of Biloxi—and bring home a personalized memento to boot. Everyone could see the foot-long moustache and dark, wild eyes and the incredibly facile hands; almost no one could see the agonized genius. Just beneath the cheap, self-inflicted, show-biz froth, the scene had the wrenching pathos of a fairground midway— "step right up and see the . . ."

Part 2: *At the Height of His Art*

Flames rushed up and out from the Bijou Oyster Saloon on the ground floor of the old two-story Swetman Building. A night watchman seeing smoke over on Pass Christian ran to sound the alarm bell at around 2:00 A.M. Before the twelve-man volunteer fire department could be roused and mustered, and the handsome though somewhat old-fashioned hand pumper hauled to the blaze, the fire had fed itself the building and was belching sparks. Within minutes the adjoining Masonic Opera House was wrapped in waves of flame and the conflagration burst out in all directions: cottages, business buildings,

Figure 12
George's domain the morning after the fire that destroyed much of Biloxi's commercial area, Friday, October 12, 1894. That's Ohr with two of his children standing near the main kiln.

shops of every kind were ablaze. The inferno engulfed a shoe store and barber shop in a building owned by George Ohr, Sr. Over twenty establishments were burning now, including a two-story cottage that belonged to him as well. At some distance from the gutted Swetman Building four more small frame structures, all owned by the senior Ohr, were aflame: one of these housed Sing Lee's Laundry, another Eikel's tailor shop, and next to catch spark and fire was the grocery store run by Mrs. Johanna Ohr. The flames ran up the tall, flat facade that gave the little building more of a presence than it deserved, up to the very top where George had balanced a row of his pots. Moments later, just behind the crumbling grocery, the famous Biloxi Art Pottery came ablaze; furious, orange-red flames jetted from the windows and lapped up the grey, weathered boards, all glowing like a great kiln stoked full with tinder.[37]

For the Ohr family the sun rose that morning (October 12, 1894) on a scene of crushing devastation: the house and everything in it was gone, the pottery was gone, everything lay in ruin. There in the rubble, posturing tall, posing for the camera, was George Edgar Ohr, a straw hat on his head, one arm properly braced on a hip, Leo and Clo at his sides, and all about the work of his youth, shattered and smoldering (Figure 12). Penniless, robbed of the treasure he would not sell, Ohr was again at a turning. A lesser spirit might have paused, but this was no tradesman who could contemplate alternatives—there were no alternatives but to rebuild and feel the wheel again.

Carefully he picked through the rubble, putting aside and gently heaping up the burned and broken bodies of his cherished artware. These were his "killed babies," and he could no more part with them than he could part with a child who had broken an arm. His sweet little Asa had died less than a year before (December 7, 1893) and that loss compounded the sorrowful analogy. Some of these charred remains of his youth would be carefully preserved for all his life, and well beyond. Frozen as they are in the flame-light of that horrible Friday (Figures 77–81), today they are an important guide to his stylistic development. To George they were the dead offspring of his younger days, and like a worn prayer book, could not simply be thrown away.

Not every pot he had made was lost in the fire. Many a jug, water bottle, pitcher, and trinket,[38] and even a few vases and ewers had found themselves to safety all around the country. A precious few other vessels brazened out the flames. The monumental unglazed vase with the skaters was away in the backyard and the water-bottle stand with the head was probably not far from it; they both survived unscathed. It seems likely that several plaster pitcher molds and even some bisque ware withstood the holocaust. But the special pieces that he coveted most were almost all in ruin. Many of them managed to remain unbroken only to have their low-fired glazes blistered black, permanently encrusted with soot and ash.

Mr. Ohr was fortunate in one regard: his pottery establishment had already become a local landmark and so he was able to quickly raise eight hundred dollars in Biloxi to rebuild. During the winter of 1894 to 1895 he oversaw the construction of a modest little house and just north of it a grand new workshop capped off with a five-story pagoda-like tower. The flagpole on the roof insured that it would be the tallest structure for miles around, something folks would have no trouble finding. As for construction, it was a simple affair, a wooden frame with boards on the outside, no

finished ceilings or plaster walls, but it did have glass windows:

Architecturally, it is chaotic, having some of the characteristics of every well-known type of building except that which it might most readily be expected to have—the low-pillared, balconied, Colonial house in which the South abounds.
The ground floor suggests a log cabin, the upper ones a cross between a Chinese pagoda and a Russian country house, the whole the dream palace of a freakish brain. Needless to say, Mr. Ohr built it himself. And he's proud of it.
The corner-stone isn't a stone at all, but a fantastically twisted log of wood suggesting the headless body of a man.[39]

Painting in bold, bright letters across the southern face he christened the building the BILOXI ART POTTERY UNLIMITED. In short order George was back in production,[40] but this time with a brilliance and creative drive that seems to have taken its energy and its urgency from the fire itself.

He had experimented before with indentations and creases, folding, crushing, and distorting a piece that was kept plastic for several days after it had come from the wheel. George had also already invented the technique for transforming the lip of an exquisitely thin-walled vase into a symmetrical succession of graceful folds; he was an unrivaled thrower and had made many vessels that were remarkably light and delicate.[41] "Certainly he could throw wares of considerable size with walls much thinner than any other potter ever has accomplished. It is quite probable that George Ohr, rated simply as a mechanic, was the most expert thrower that the craft has ever known."[42] And early on, having probably accidently chipped the rim of a piece, he boldly and deliberately made chipping a decorative device. Still, what remains of the prefire work on the whole seems relatively reserved. In a strange way the fire may well have been fortuitous: the flames burned away the old and quickened the growth of the new. It didn't happen all at once, but soon enough Ohr was pushing the bounds of restraint with both hands: reticulating, folding, pinching, twisting, easing the thin clay into new visual rhythms

Figure 13
The Biloxi Art Pottery Unlimited, c. 1898.

that captured a thrilling vitality and excitement, a *vis viva*.

When the resident poet-philosopher of Biloxi wasn't making pots he was painting signs chiding, admonishing, challenging, welcoming, and lecturing the world. An invitation to come visit the pottery, lettered on a huge signboard, swung at the corner of the street and beneath it a verse:

The poet sings in dainty rhymes
Of summer days and sunny climes;
* Of beauteous maidens, passing fair,*
* With witching eyes and wavy hair.*
Turn near the end and you're apt to C
A welcome to the Pot-ohr-e[43]

A long slender bit of unbridled bravado was wedged in place at the southeast corner of the building under the overhanging porch. Modestly it proclaimed, -UNEQUALED.-UNRIVALED. UNDISPUTED.-GREATEST.-ART POTTER. ON EARTH. In time the edge of that porch itself became one long wrapped-around sign: GEORGE E. OHR, DELIEATOR IN ART POTTERY; MAGNUM OPUS, NULLI SECUNDUS, OPTIMUS COGITO, ERGO SUM. And just over the door, ERECTED IN 1888, BURNED OUT AND REBUILT IN 1894 BY THE UNEQUALED VARIETY POTTER, CRANK, ETC. The use of the word *crank* was explained by a contemporary interviewer: "Mr. Ohr says that he believes firmly in majority rule. The majority of people in Biloxi think he has wheels [in his head], so he considers it only fair to intimate as much to the general public."[44]

To attract attention George had created the Mad Potter persona, but it was, like all life's masquerades, no more real than that. It came easily to him, and despite that natural predisposition to the part and the liberated delight with which he took advantage of it (for Mr. Ohr could be rude and mischievous), he was assuredly not "crazy." The people who knew him, knew him to be egocentric, "a show off," at times thoughtless and self-indulgent. He was, if anything, nonconformist-mad, artist-mad, genius-mad, hardly mad-mad, and he so enjoyed the game. "I found out long ago that it paid me to act this way," George once confided, his black eyes smiling.[45]

The Cotton States and International Exposition opened at Piedmont Park in Atlanta, Georgia, at sundown on Wednesday, September 18, 1895. President Grover Cleveland touched an electric key in his library at Gray Gables, a resulting sharp metallic click sounded in Atlanta, and that was immediately followed by cheering and the simultaneous thunder of a hundred cannon. The self-proclaimed "greatest art potter on Earth," never one to miss a fair provided it wasn't too expensive to get to, found himself a spot on the midway over by the merry-go-round near the Jackson Street entrance. His modest booth was east of the Monkey Paradise and the Ostrich Farm, not far from the Rocky Mountain Ponies.[46] From where he set out his wares he could see the Phoenix (Ferris) Wheel and might even have heard the gunfire whenever Buffalo Bill's Wild West kicked up dust in the Grand Stand. George wasn't listed among the official displayers (there were six thousand exhibits), but there he was anyway and he brought along a young assistant, a Mr. H. J. Portman (that's Harry on the right in Figure 14).

Portman was raised by the Ohr family, and George, who regarded the boy as a foster son, taught him the potter's trade. Being an artistic fellow, Harry painted signs and occasionally

Figure 14
Ohr at the Cotton States and International Exposition in Atlanta, 1895. Harry Portman, who assisted at the pottery from around 1895 until about 1907, stands on the right.

CLAY NOVELTIES.
CONN

The Artistic Souvenirs
Made here. are the work of
GEO. E. OHR.
The Biloxi
Mississippi POTTER.

FAC-SIMILE
OLD STYLE PITCHERS

Machinery Bld" Atlanta Exposition

Figure 15
Ohr, his moustache wrapped around
his ears, performing on the wheel at the
Machinery Building in Atlanta, 1895.
A number of pots seem to be covered
with rags, probably damp, to keep
them from drying too fast.

modeled decorations, sprigging them onto
pieces George had made. More often he decorated molded puzzle jugs—molding may have
been his speciality. Though he seems never to
have worked the wheel he did build things
with clay, such as knickknack shelves and the
like. Every now and then Harry produced some
charming incised designs and even did a little
under-the-glaze slip painting, but the scarcity
of faience carrying Portman's mark (a conjoined JHP or simple H.P.) suggests that he
rarely worked on the thrown artware. There
certainly were plenty of other things for him to
do around he shop, and he stayed on for a
number of years.[47]

Even before Ohr had come to the midway in
Atlanta, to that ramshackle shack decorated in
checkerboard oilcloth, he had already made the
giant leap in imagination that would enable
him in just a few years to create a new ceramic
art. At his feet on the dirt road were a half-
dozen old standbys: molded pitchers, like the
Tarpon on the right, the Steamboat, and the
Musical Cherubs. And as expected there were a
few of his bibelots,[48] as well: a realistic ceramic
conch shell and a tiny cabin. But among these
essentially commercial products were five
rather interesting "mud fixens," which presage
some of his revolutionary work of the last years
of the century. One (at his right) has been

twisted, top against bottom, creating a body of vertically spiraling pleats. Another has its rim folded and its sides indented. A third is a delightfully original arched-conical form with a long neck and tall pedestal base. One (on his left) shows a tightly controlled scalloped rim playing off against a matching band of indentations. And the last rather ordinary looking piece (just in front of him) is his much belabored Peach Blown vase, a supposed duplicate of a famous Chinese porcelain[49] that underscores his mastery of glaze. Though Ohr made much of this particular vase it's really rather homely, looking very little like the pink-to-yellow skin of a peach and even less like the Chinese porcelain. Still he did accomplish the extraordinary effect of a gradated glaze thinning in hue, albeit from an unattractive olive-brown to the clear yellow-orange of the body.

It appears that the Biloxi Mississippi Potter also had a little booth indoors in the Machinery Building (Figure 15) where he sold his "clay novelties," offered "the Finest Assortment of After Dinner Cups in Atlanta," and made "Artistic Souvenirs" right in front of your eyes. Ohr had come with a large selection of delicate demitasse cups and wafer-thin matching saucers that must have been quite popular. With Portman watching over the affairs of the Biloxi Mississippi Art and Novelty Pottery back on the midway, George could sell a different line of wares in the Machinery Building several blocks away. The Atlanta Exposition lasted only a few months, ending on December 31, 1895, and George Ohr, M.D., (he occasionally added that title, explaining that it stood for Mud Dauber) returned home.

He had apparently done quite well, winning some sort of prize at the fair.[50] Thus encouraged, the new year began on a positive note. By then the response to George's one-man show had moved him into the pale spotlight of a minor celebrity, even inspiring a rather dreadful novel called *The Wonderful Wheel* (1896).[51] Its main character was a "hoodoo" southern potter "with strange, flashing, black eyes, and a black mustache so long that he draped it over his ears when he worked." A potter who "made queerly-shaped jugs and vases, and mugs which poured the water out when you were not expecting it."

For the Pot-Ohr 1896 was a productive year from both a commercial and, far more importantly, an artistic standpoint. One of the practical things he tackled at that time was the creation of several new molds—possibly to make up for losses in the fire of 1894. In any event, in 1896 he produced plaster molds for long, medium, and short pouring spouts, dated March 4, March 4, and November 20 respectively. The bodies of his marvelous coffeepots and teapots were always thrown, but their graceful serpentine spouts were best molded separately. Moreover the large, early pitchers like the Tarpon[52] (which most probably predated the fire) were made by forcing clay into the mold impression by hand from the inside. They came into the world without handles and Ohr had been making a variety of new handle molds starting April 4, 1895, soon after the pottery had been rebuilt.

Both the Tarpon and Steamboat pitchers carried simple local scenes sculptured in a flattened, crude, though charming country style that was typical of his work. They're wonderful examples of nineteenth-century American folk art. The same kind of modeling appears in miniature on a set of brazenly bawdy ceramic tokens, each of which has a sophomoric raised rebus on both sides (Figure 95). These were facsimile brothel coins in the ancient Roman tradition. And given the robust trade going on in the sporting houses in the notorious Storyville district of New Orleans, matters of the bagnio were a natural source of local humor. It's easy to imagine George, a devilish smile on his face, pressing one of these little molded bits of mischief into the hand of some unsuspecting victim. For whatever bizarre reason he produced these tokens of the lupanar, he certainly must have anticipated a considerable demand for them: he made hundreds—all unsigned.

Though his molded wares were inexpensive to produce and appear to have sold well, the genre did not always seem to bring out the best in Happy George. In fact he became increasingly pragmatic when it came to producing molds. He certainly was not above casting them directly from any object that took his fancy, and had been doing that unceremoniously for

Figure 16
Molded Tarpin pitcher, c. 1889–98. Private collection, New York.

Figure 17
Seashell planter, c. 1895. Private collection, New York.

Figure 18
The inside of the Pot-Ohr-E; the
picture dates from around the spring of
1896.

years—a remolded doorstop survived the fire of
1894, and there's a lion's head boss that was
first a glass paperweight. A milk-glass
knickknack of a woman's hand holding a bird
(patented, August 1889) served as the model for
a mold that subsequently produced ceramic
inkwells. Indeed a mold exists that was
obviously formed by simply pouring plaster
onto a cut-glass bowl. He seems even to have
made molds of crabs and sea shells directly
from the real thing, creating several delightful
works in the process. After a while George
began producing a number of smaller rather
sophisticated "fac-simile old style pitchers,"
which were much more ambitious in their
sculptural decoration and much more
derivative in their inspiration and execution. In
short whenever he felt the need, improper
George simply swiped what he fancied: he
thought nothing of using a handsome pressed-
glass pitcher and a bit of plaster to produce a
supply of molded earthenware clones.[53]
Though he did introduce several new pitchers
that year, including a fine one carrying the
likeness of Grover Cleveland (April 17, 1896),
molding would not serve as a vehicle for his
craft very much longer.

The shop was starting to fill in nicely by early
1896 even though the Greatest Variety Potter in
the World had already begun lining the shelved
wooden fences that bounded the property with
hundreds of pieces of artware—perhaps to keep
them out of harm's way should fire strike the
building. Mugs and pitchers hung from nails in
the ceiling beams and the sagging shelves carried a joyous clutter of creation, "no two alike."

On March 18, 1896, showman George had a
visitor to the shop he would always remember.
On that dreary day, big as life, who should
walk in the door but Mr. Joseph Jefferson: *the*
Joe Jefferson who had thrilled audiences across
the country with his unforgettable portrayals of
Caleb Plummer, Bob Acres, Dr. Ollapod, Dr.
Pangloss, Mr. Golightly, Huge de Brass, and of
course, the ever popular Rip Van Winkle. He
had, as one contemporary put it, "an exceptional hold upon the heart and imagination of
his time."[54] In due course the greatest variety
actor in the world was handed a pin and a
damp pot and invited to add an immortal inscription. What came out was Rip Van Winkle's
then already famous toast, "Here's your good
health and your family's and may they all have
long lives and prosper." By now the better half
of Rip-incarnate was outside in the buggy
"constantly interrupting: 'Hurry up, Joe! It's
going to rain'."[55] Ohr, who had a broad child-
like streak, was so thrilled by the visit that he
put the grail in a place of honor and proceeded
to engrave those memorable words and date, in
a facsimile Jeffersonian hand, on almost everything he made that day.[56]

Newcomb College had moved to expanded
quarters back in 1891 and the art department
moved with it. In the boiler room of the new
building they installed kilns and wheels for the
making of pottery. The first professional potter
hired was a Frenchman named Jules Gabry
who had worked in Cannes and later traveled to
Brazil. He was already elderly when he came to
New Orleans and did not stay long at Newcomb.
By then the need for the Baronne Street operation had faded and when Gabry's successor
departed after only a short while, J. F. Meyer
became potter at Newcomb (probably in the
second half of 1896), a job he would hold with
distinction the rest of his long life. During the

period from 1895 through the next two decades Newcomb was a center of the Arts and Crafts Movement in the United States. Along with firms like Rookwood, Grueby, and (after 1901) Van Briggle, it was one of the major commercial producers of American art pottery.

As for Mr. Ohr, although he was creating his finest art, things weren't going smoothly financially. The flasks, pudding molds, flowerpots, drainpipes, and such, sold well enough but there wasn't much money to be made in that. The competition with glass bottles, tin cans, and inexpensive white tableware had already changed the industry and these were lean times for most. Besides, George was a neglectful, terribly bad shopkeeper who wouldn't interrupt "a conversation with the shabbiest person displaying an interest in his work"[57] to sell a flue pipe to some neighbor who didn't care a bit about art. Nor was he particularly willing to part with his artware. "Occasionally he turns out a few bits for visitors to snatch at as souvenirs, but not unless necessity compels him to do so. On some piece that strikes his fancy he will put a fabulous price."[58] A decorative mug might be handsomely tagged at five dollars, a vase at twenty-five dollars and much more; the high prices were a measure of the potential buyer's commitment to and appreciation of Ohr's art. Only "if you become communicative, and rave a bit over some of the finer bits of faience"[59] will you endear yourself to the potter and even have a chance of taking home something special. George had no desire to part with what he valued, and no interest in selling what he didn't; in all, hardly a strategy for success. But George didn't seem depressed by the modesty of his circumstances: "Every genius is in debt," he quipped.[60]

The birth of Oto T. Ohr on September 11, 1895, had given him four children to feed and made the lure of moonlighting even more appealing. Meyer was in New Orleans and if George worked a bit for him, especially in the off-season, he could spend even more time in Biloxi on his art and less fretting over flue pipe. Besides, New Orleans was such a great place for a man like him to visit. As tradition has it, George Edgar Ohr, at the height of his artistic powers, supposedly returned to the big city to work at

the flourishing Newcomb Pottery.[51] The incomparable genius, the superb innovator, was again assistant to Uncle Joe at the wheel of tradition.

Mr. Ohr knew and liked Monsieur Gabry and it's possible that both of them may even have assisted Meyer for a time at Newcomb.[62] In any event, George invited the old gentleman "to share his daily bread, and his potter's clay."[63] It was probably around 1897 that Gabry packed his meager belongings and made the journey to Biloxi, but he was already despondent and didn't remain long. It's not clear what happened next, but he seems to have committed "SUISIDE in Biloxi's water—August 18th, 1897," as attested to by inscriptions on several of Ohr's pots. When the old man was gone his potter's wheel was carefully hauled up to the foot of the last flight of stairs leading to the sunny roof of the pagoda. George had a strong sense of history and stored the ancient kick-wheel in the corner where it would be safe.

It is not known when the Blacksmith Potter was in New Orleans, but each sojourn must have been brief. With the easy availability of freight trains, our free spirit could have come and gone over the next several years whenever he felt the

Figure 19
The potter and his wares, c. 1897.

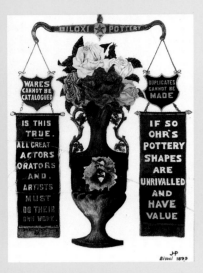

Figure 20
A painting on glass by Portman, 1899.

Figure 21
A display of some of Ohr's best pots, probably spring 1899 but definitely prior to June 1899.

need to earn a little extra cash. In any event, like Meyer he would have only worked during the spring and fall semesters and been off the whole summer. It is known that George was in Biloxi in early 1897 because he was visited by the editor of the *Brick,* a trade periodical that subsequently carried a rather complimentary two-page story called "A Biloxi Pottery."[64] Ohr was at home in early 1898 too, when Josephine became pregnant with Flo Lucagina (who was born on December 11, 1898, and died before her second birthday). It's quite revealing, though, that for whatever time he did spend at Newcomb, for whatever energy he did invest, there does not seem to be a single one of their vases bearing his mark, or even the slightest trace of his aesthetic influence. And that's all the more ironic, since at that very moment Mr. Ohr was undoubtedly the greatest potter on earth. Family legend has it that picaresque George was ultimately asked to leave the prim and proper portals of H. Sophie Newcomb Memorial College, it would seem, for conduct unbecoming a potter to decorous young ladies. Though no documentation exists on the affair, that part of the oral tradition rings true enough.

George really was a fun-loving character, whose sexuality bubbled up in the sensuality of his work. Occasionally less restrained, he was led to the raucous edges of good taste by an adolescent sense of humor that betrayed him at every turn. What resulted was anachronistic nineteenth-century Funk: a sculptured bisque breast, a vulvate slit coin bank incised with hairlike strokes—perhaps for the benefit of the blind (Figure 94). There is a story of a local justice of the peace, Orin Davidson, a friend and admirer, who one day brought home a piece of Biloxi bawdryware to add to his collection of Ohr's work. The judge's more sober wife insisted that he immediately remove "that thing" from the house. The glazed phallus promptly vanished, probably returned to its grinning maker—George and the judge must have had a good laugh. One of Ohr's favorite fair trinkets, one that he made by hand in great abundance, was a small glazed turdefied chamber pot.[65] Even before that tasteless bit of whimsy, he had produced scatological jokes in the form of appropriately lifelike pads of mock animal ordure, which might be placed on a rug or under a chair for the delight and amusement of all.

The notion of Ohr freight-hopping back and forth to Newcomb is not precluded by the fact that dated examples of his own artware exist from 1895 through 1907,[66] inclusively. For example, in 1897 a yellow fever epidemic swept Biloxi and George was there with his family. He left a poignant record of it on the bottom of a pot: *Mad[e] during the Yellow Jack Scare Sept. 12, 1897.* A six-inch bowl carries across its bisque face the inscription: *Mad[e] in the Presence of my Dear great Mama Dec. 14-8 pm 1898.* Always the devoted fan of Mr. J. Jefferson, Ohr made a large plaque (10½ by 10½ inches) dated 1898 depicting Joe's Buzzards Bay, Massachusetts, residence.

Still, the links with Meyer were strong and long-lived. That the two old friends often came in contact with each other during this period (in Biloxi and at Newcomb) is at least suggested by a molded bisque pitcher with Ohr's Biloxi mark, dated 1899, which is identical to a glazed specimen marked *Jos. F. Meyer, the Pottery Club, 249 Baronne Street, N. O., La.* In any event, George liked to travel and it is known from at least three of his pots, also carrying the overlapping script *F-S* mark of Susan Frackelton, along with the inscribed date *'99,* that Ohr probably visited Milwaukee, Wisconsin, that year.

Folk potters often scrawled their names and dates across their work, and Pennsylvania redware pots inscribed with verse date back to the 1750s. Having been inspired to do the same by his encounter with Jefferson, George slowly began to appreciate and explore the artistic-communicative possibilities of the device. All his life he was a man who used language as freely as he used clay; after a day's work he'd often stay up late into the night typing poems, long letters, and bits of philosophical wisdom. Writing on a piece of ceramic seemed to give permanence to the words, and that appealed to him. A multicolored vase is hand lettered all around its body:

With Earth's first Clay they did the Last man
  knead
And there of the last Harvest sow'd the Seed
  And the first Morning of Creation wrote
What the last Dawn of Reckoning Shall read.

  Omar Khayyam
Dito Pot. Ohr E George   Biloxi -4–1–1899.[67]

Always the bad boy, George inscribed a brown, two-handled mug with this bit of sophisticated humor: "A HOT TOMOLY! While we were on the beach indulging in nature's folly the sun got 2 my back while the sand was Hot To Molly's."

But his most elaborate use of "wordart" is a large umbrella stand dated *Dec–18–1900* that he created for the Smithsonian Institution but never bothered to deliver. Its entire surface serves as a canvas for a sociopolitical statement in the form of a touching letter sent to him by a friend who had been forced to leave Biloxi for speaking out on behalf of a "fearless paper." The editor of the newspaper in question was subsequently murdered. This fascinating time capsule is further adorned with a wonderful commentary, a bit of philosophy in verse from the Blacksmith Potter (the entire text is included herein on p. 178).

Part 3: *High Art At Biloxi*

"High Art at Biloxi, Miss." was the title of an article that supposedly appeared in a New York newspaper of December 22, 1898.[68] In the main it was an overly clever reaction to a provocative handbill that Ohr had recently circulated. Even so it underscored the extent of the notoriety the brash Biloxian had already begun to engender. The reporter was moved to unrestrained sarcasm by George's familiar "touching modesty" and homey candor: "American born, free and patriotic, blowing my own bugle, and will tackle the greatest of all great potters in the world, creating shapes on ceramic wheel." "The twisted, crinkled clomerations in my Art Pottery stand alone on earth—I cannot duplicate such myself." The braggadocio was actually quite specific, and quite revealing: creating extraordinary shapes on the wheel was becoming Ohr's primary focus despite the fact that his better glazes were absolutely spectacular.

William A. King, the well-known art critic writing for the *Illustrated Buffalo Express,* requested a copy of that circular and Ohr replied by way of explanation: "I am making pottery

for art sake, God sake, the future generation, and—by present indications—for my own satisfaction, but when I'm gone (like Palissy) my work will be prized, honored and cherished." Already there in his voice is a distant whisper of despair behind the blind confidence that comes well rationalized, however justified. "I enclose," he went on, "one of my 'get up' [handbills] which will give you a synopsis of the who, where from, where 2 and so on of the Biloxi M.D. (mud dauber) and P.M. (pot maker)."[69] King very sympathetically reported that Ohr had, to date accumulated "upwards of 6,000 or 7,000 pieces, no two of which are just alike in shape and decoration." And he astutely recognized that "there is art— real art—in the Biloxian's pottery."[70]

Figure 22
Harry Portman and George Ohr posing for the camera sometime in 1899.

The brouhaha was picked up in the trade publications where some of Ohr's pots were duly pictured, his history briefly summarized, and his name brought to the notice of the community of professionals. The April 1899 issue of the *China, Glass and Pottery Review* showed George in his studio-shop and reported him as saying: "According to the Good Book, we are created from clay, and as Nature had it so destined that no two of us are alike, all couldn't be

symmetrically formed, caused a variety to be wabble-jawed, hare-lipped, cross-eyed, all colors, bow-legged, knock-kneed, extra limbs, also minus of the same, all sizes from 30 inches to 75 ditto. Everyone of us sees different, has a different voice, and don't all like cabbage or chew tobacco!" The God-clay-man-clay image always with him, he continued: "I make disfigured pottery—couldn't and wouldn't if I could make it any other way." Ohr's art is boldly fixed at the extreme of chance, spontaneity, natural asymmetry, calculated imperfection, rustic vigor, wit, and mischief. The June issue of the same periodical pictured him posing with Portman (Figure 22) and reminding us that "we are from clay."

The Mad Potter was the consummate craftsman who transcended craft, and, like none before him, became an artist struggling to express his humanity in the clay. He was the Romantic spirit translating ephemeral passion into palpable form—this with an intensity and sureness of hand guided by intuition and borne on cosmic egocentricity. Unshackled from the dulling influence of communal acceptance, self-sustained on high purpose and singular conviction, energized by attention if not adoration, the lone potter from Biloxi could go anywhere his creative imagination would lead. Unafraid of the bizarre, indeed allied with it, he masterfully worked the clay until it had the plasticity of molten glass, coaxing it into shapes never before conceived. Most were then bathed in superb glazes, many marvelously complex and innovative, and all formulated himself.[71] But Ohr was already (around late 1898) beginning to articulate what would become the guiding principle of his later years—that glaze effects were the accident of the fire, and that shape was all. "Shapes come to the potter as verses come to the poet. Clay follows the fingers and the fingers follow the mind." "My creations have an intrinsic value in shape."

In the summer of 1899 the proprietor of the Biloxi Art and Novelty Pottery crated up eight pieces of his ware—a miniature ceramic tattered hat, two folded bowls, four lovely vases, a delicate handled cup with "copper red splashes"—and sent them off, an unsolicited gift to the Smithsonian and the people of America.[72] These were small pots (the tallest only 4¾ inches), not his most splendid creations, but still quite fine. Besides, they made the point that needed making by showing the range of his prodigious talent and extraordinary aesthetic. And so George carefully packed them up and shipped them off, as always with an eye to the future. He had no way of knowing that these little mud babies would be kept out of sight and treated carelessly for well over half a century. They were not even formally accessioned until eighty-seven years later and by then every one of them was already damaged: the black crystalline bowl was cracked, the greenish yellow one shattered, the handle broken from the cup, and all were chipped.

The exhibition of American ceramics held at the National Arts Club around January 1900 brought together the work of many of the nation's most prominent potteries. The large green-gray room, lined with shelves and cabinets, was well lighted and provided an ideal setting. Over a dozen finely painted Rookwood vases were in one case, while the massive, monochrome Grueby vessels seemed more suited to standing on the floor here and there around the room. A small tabletop held a group of irides-

cent bowls and vases by the studio potter Theophilus Brouwer of East Hampton, New York. A long shelf displayed the pieces from Newcomb College, while another just above it held vessels by Charles Volkmar. Some interesting work by the Dedham Pottery was there as well, along with the wares of several other manufactories. Tiles and chargers hung on the walls and there was even a fine selection of the lustres of Massier's Golfe Juan pottery in France. "George H. Ohr, of Biloxi, Mississippi, showed some quaint potteries that reminded one of the ancient Aztecs," wrote the reviewer for *Keramic Studio*. "But the quaintest thing about him is his huge conceit. He adds a card with some legend inscribed to every piece, one of which describes himself as the only one and greatest variety potter in the world, or words to that effect."[73] Pot-Ohr-E-George had not endeared himself to the keepers of good taste.

The Paris Exposition Universelle of 1900, which opened on April 14, may have started out as an embodiment of peace and progress but between the anarchists and the Dreyfus Affair the City of Light had lost its sparkle to many, especially the crowned heads of Europe who stayed away en masse. Still, fifty-one million visitors came to the fair where they could see the latest work of almost every important pottery in Europe and America. There were a total of 139 exhibitors from the United States showing artistic ceramics. The Rookwood Pottery, which took a grand prize, a gold medal, and a silver medal, had a major presence, having spent eighty-seven hundred dollars on expenses alone; Grueby Faience Company was there too, and its one-hundred-piece representation won one silver and two gold medals. Maria Storer and Susan Frackelton (who won a bronze medal) each also had their own displays.

A large number of contributors were china painters and their efforts constituted the collective exhibition of the National League of Mineral Painters. The league also sponsored a showing of the works of several outstanding American potteries and potters: the Newcomb Pottery of New Orleans (awarded a bronze medal); Mary Louise McLaughlin of Cincinnati; Linna Irelan of San Francisco; Hugh Robertson of Dedham, Massachusetts (awarded

Figure 24
A porcelain souvenir plate showing the pottery, made by a European firm for T. A. Iler of Biloxi. Private collection, New York.

Figure 25
The Blacksmith Potter in the backyard of his shop. The brick face of the large kiln is behind him to the north and a stack of cut wood for the fire is at his left.

a bronze medal); Charles Volkmar of Corona, New York; and George E. Ohr of Biloxi, Mississippi.[74] The American potters who won recognition, like their European counterparts, did not stray far from tradition, avoiding the "feverish" and "eccentric" in favor of the moderate and tasteful. Where that left Mr. Ohr was obvious: he was adrift on his own, sixty years out of time. Understandably enough he did not win any medals, though someone must have been quite impressed with his work because George later did receive an order for several pieces from a collector in Paris.[75]

By the beginning of the new century Ohr had achieved a position of some national prominence, often being included in the company of the major potters of the country. The January 1901 issue of the *Art Interchange,* "an illustrated monthly magazine for artists" published in New York, carried a most laudatory article entitled "Biloxi Pottery." The writer reported that "the potter dreams of fame, not riches. He cares not that each piece of work will find a ready buyer, that is not his idea. But while he turns the wheel he is dreaming of the day when the whole will be sold intact. . . . His work has an art and a grace of its own that must be recognized."[76]

Interestingly, the photo Ohr provided for this article shows ten brilliantly configured unglazed pieces. The picture survives (Figure 107) and around its uncropped margin Ohr had scrawled "Colors or quality counts *nothing* in my creations! God put no color or quality in souls." By "quality" he apparently meant surface characteristics apart from color. Consistently inconsistent, he went on to glaze several of those very pieces, but it's also clear that he felt they could stand on their shapes alone, glazeless.[77]

When the Providence Art Club of Rhode Island mounted its major Arts and Crafts exhibition (March 19 to April 13) of 1901, it featured fine examples of pottery along with bookbinding, stained glass, wood carving, embroidery, leather goods, and metalwork. Many of the leading American ceramics firms were represented at that prestigious gathering, including the Biloxi Art Pottery Unlimited. The Mad Potter had sixteen pieces of his artware on view alongside Tiffany's display of Favrile vases and stained-glass windows, books from the Roycrofters, and Mucha posters. The show was enthusiastically reviewed, but this time the writer for *Keramic Studio* didn't even mention Ohr.[78]

The main event of the year was the Pan-American Exposition held in Buffalo, New York, from May to November of 1901. It wasn't a global fair, but instead focused on promoting the interests of the countries of the Western Hemisphere. The exhibit of Arts and Crafts was prominently featured in the central court of the imposing Manufactures and Liberal Arts Building. Mr. William King, who by then was referring to George as "my friend Ohr," was a member of the Exposition's Committee on Fine Arts, and in May of 1901 he wrote an article describing the ceramics that would be at the fair.[79] In due course he briefly mentioned Rookwood, Grueby, Frackelton, Volkmar, and Newcomb. And then he wrote, "We will not only have an exhibit of Biloxi pottery, but we may have the Biloxi potter in person; and if we do, Pan-American visitors will see a genius who has no counterpart in the pottery world at home or abroad." A long letter written by George then followed, along with a photo of "a group of American pottery" showing a few mud babies in among the jars and vases of this country's most revered producers.

Again the prizes were won by Rookwood and Grueby (both took golds), and Newcomb (which won a silver medal). Mary McLaughlin and Charles Volkmar each won bronze medals, the two remaining awards in the pottery category.[80] It doesn't seem (at least from the literature) that George ever actually went to Buffalo; he might have been there, but he didn't win any medals, or even honorable mention.[81] Still, the entire event was soon overshadowed by the single act of a young anarchist, who turned the exposition into a national tragedy. On September 6 Leon Czolgosz walked up to President McKinley, who was shaking hands on a reception line. Holding a hidden pistol in a handkerchief, he fired twice, point-blank; the president of the United States, mortally wounded, died eight days later.

When Edwin Atlee Barber produced the second edition of his already classic tome, *The Pottery and Porcelain of the United States* (1901), he added several new selections, one of which began: "The pottery of George E. Ohr, at Biloxi, Miss., is, in some respects, one of the most interesting in the United States . . . . the principal beauty of the ware lies in the richness of some of the glazes, which present great variety in coloring. . . . Singularly enough, he [Ohr] claims more merit for his shapes than for any other feature." Dr. Barber pictured three pieces of Biloxi artware—two finely glazed examples and one charming little "entirely unglazed" vase.[82] Ohr also sent W. A. King an assortment of his work and included therein several "quaintly distorted unglazed pieces." These were not unfinished wares, but instead a sample of an important facet of the complete work of the great innovator, a silent statement of an aesthetic of quintessential form.[83]

The *Crockery and Glass Journal* published several short articles about Ohr, as well as a long rather forthright letter from him dated June 1901. Once more he set out the two themes that dominated his philosophy: he would not sell his work piecemeal, and the primary merit of that work was its originality of form. Again he exposed his frustration and his growing resentment: "My 20 years ability is indorsed on my work. But my name is mud at Present as to merits or collecting. . . . Well! if my name wont

Count now the other part cant Be respected—and that is equal to throwing Pearl to Pigs"[84] The idea of keeping his oeuvre intact is one Ohr struggled with all his life, perhaps because it was and still is so alien to the way things are done yet it's so terribly reasonable. As he put it: "To distribute what I have [left of my life's work] is like distributing a poets work—by giving hundreds of lines too hundreds of creatures—hundreds of miles apart. . . . As I cant eat what I have in pottery my object is dispose of the whole collection to one creature or one country!" Clearly, he could not sell his art one mud baby at a time and have it scattered, the gestalt lost forever—it had to be sold (he needed the money), and so logic demanded he sell it all at once. What did it matter that there were no takers—it was the only course, and George was a single-minded man.

He was glazing fewer pieces now but still worked as he had always, essentially alone, doing almost everything himself, by hand. Speaking

Figure 26
The Ohr parlor, which was painted in tones of orange and blue in the manner of the Egyptians. Note George's reflection in the mirror.

warmly of his father, Oto recalled those days years later (at age 86):

When he worked on the pedal wheel, I remember him saying "There's ten thousand pieces here, and no two pieces alike." He'd make one kind of jar, and he'd change it for the next. Maybe he'd put one handle on it—two, three, or four handles on it.

I do remember how he worked the clay. He'd hook the horse onto the wagon and take the ferry across the back bay, dig his own clay, work the sand out of it. He'd be gone three days sometimes with that horse and wagon—to find clay that was suitable for him. I don't know where he slept—in the wagon or somewhere.

He dried the clay in a pit in the yard that he poured concrete into. We'd go out and watch him, sitting on the steps or in his chair. He'd put so much clay in there and so much water, and let it set. The sand went to the bottom, the clay would be five to ten inches thick. He'd scoop that up in his shovel and put it in his bucket and carry it into the shop where he had his kiln—where it would finish drying out. He slow fired it for two or three days—just enough to absorb the water out of it. Then he'd beat it into balls and throw it on the wheel—a foot outfit.

He made his own glaze out of different ingredients, and painted this stuff four or five colors. If he wanted a streak, he'd paint it; whatever would come to his mind, he'd put it on that piece of pottery. He'd never let me work on it, because I was too little then.

My father was born with that kind of gift. I thought he was a pretty wise man. The townspeople thought he didn't have no sense—that he was crazy. He looked like a wild man at times. He'd let his hair grow and he wouldn't shave. He'd take his long hair and tie it in a knot in the back of his head. In other words, he was living his own life, the way he wanted to live it. He was a wise man the good Lord sent down here to make stuff and show the world.[85]

By the turn of the century the Blacksmith Potter was already a figure to be contended with, one way or another, a figure whose own verbal excesses unhappily invited derision. The ceramist William Jervis (himself barely competent on the wheel), writing in his *Encyclopedia of Ceramics* (1902), pointed out that George was

"laying up at Biloxi a vast store of ware in the hopes that it may be purchased entire by the nation."[86] Rather than dealing with the aesthetic issues raised by Ohr, Jervis simply went on to dismiss him with condescending wisecracks. Established potters like Jervis, Rhead, and Binns,[87] who were committed by their own work to tradition, rarely had anything good to say about the chief iconoclast in their ranks.[88] When Isabel McDougall wrote her report, "Some Recent Arts and Crafts Work," for *House Beautiful* in July, 1903, she no doubt felt obligated to mention Pot-Ohr-E-George even if she knew little about him—but the interior of his house was never filled with "monkey jars" as she claimed. Regarding his artware the lady rightly wrote that Ohr "sometimes disconcerts serious folk like the managers of exhibitions by filling out the blank space for price with 'worth their weight in gold.'"[89]

At forty-seven, surrounded by an incomparable body of work and convinced that it was indeed worth its weight in gold, George Edgar Ohr yearned for appreciation and recognition, for the simple affirmation that all those lonely years were somehow justified. Ironically he never seemed aware that his own demanding philosophy was an insuperable barrier to the success he now began so desperately to long for. If only America could see his art it would be taken up in its entirety, a single work in ten thousand parts, a man's life. And yet he knew he might well wait forever for some powerful aesthete to find the way to Biloxi to save the treasure en masse and vindicate the Mad Potter. George had been attracting attention in the press, but what he really needed was an opportunity to show off his best work in a place filled with important people—center stage at a major world's fair would do nicely. In a way Ohr had begun his career at the New Orleans World's Industrial and Cotton Centennial Exposition back in 1884, extended it at the Atlanta Exposition in 1895, and now he hoped to culminate it at the St. Louis fair.

The Louisiana Purchase International Exposition was held in St. Louis, Missouri, from April 30 to December 1, 1904. It celebrated the centenary of the purchase of the Louisiana Territory and was conceived on a grand scale: triple the

Figure 27
The ramshackled scuppernong grape arbor just beyond the kiln in the backyard of the pottery. The tall boy is Leo and the picture dates from around early 1902.

size of the Paris Exposition Universelle of 1900 and ten times larger than the Pan-American Exposition in Buffalo. Unlike any fair in the past, no artificial distinction was made between arts and crafts objects of excellence and traditional "fine art." Here the emphasis was more appropriately on the work of the individual artists rather than the pottery firms they represented, and that egalitarianism had a liberating effect.

By registering in the Department of Fine Arts, pottery could be displayed in the majestic Palace of Fine Arts. Sixty-seven ceramists (associated with eighteen companies and clubs) exhibited their art there, taking eighteen of the forty-eight medals garnered in applied arts at the fair. The list of American potters and decorators represented, and subsequently bemedaled, was a *Who's Who* of the Arts and Crafts Movement at its zenith: Hugh Robertson of Dedham took the grand prize, Addison Le Boutillier (Grueby's chief designer) won a gold medal, Artus and Anne Van Briggle were awarded a gold and two bronze medals, and on and on. Joseph Meyer, representing Newcomb Pottery, won a silver medal for two pieces enameled in experimental green and red metallic glazes.

The major pottery producers with plenty of wares to show staged exhibits in several buildings at once. Thus when Mr. G. E. Ohr unloaded his crates, hung out his signs, and set up his display in the far reaches of the Mines and Metallurgy Building he found himself in the company of exhibits by Rookwood, Van Briggle, and Newcomb. "He went up there with perhaps extravagant hopes, and with many hundreds of quaint and ingenious shapes in clay."[90] The jury, at least, had little trouble recognizing the outstanding merit of Ohr's work and they granted him a silver medal. But that triumph would become tempered in bitterness before the fair was over.

George had brought a good deal of artware with him and expected to sell some of those pieces to an appropriately admiring and appreciative audience of connoisseurs who would show their good taste by their willingness to pay his price. Instead he found himself in a vast

bazaar crowded with sightseers munching peanuts and candy and carrying kids—ordinary folks on holiday, come to the fair for a day's sport. None of them could even consider spending a fews weeks' salary on a weird vessel hawked by a wild-eyed, short-tempered, Mississippi crank. One can only imagine the verbal exchanges that must have taken place—the Mad Potter, growing less amusing and less amused, no doubt kept himself busy throwing

Figure 28
G. E. Ohr and his mother, a year or two before her death in 1904.

33

minor little pots, as was his wont.[91] This was the Mines and Metallurgy Building after all, and if there were cognoscenti afoot in St. Louis they were over at the Art Palace.

In the end Ohr didn't sell a single piece of art pottery "because, he said, nobody really appreciated it. They were not willing to pay enough for it. It was art, high art, he considered, almost priceless."[92] Disheartened and quite impoverished, he hadn't even the cash to ship his crates back to Biloxi and had to remain in St. Louis with them. George "went to work teaching how to make pottery, until he made enough money to return home, bringing with him the great boxes of his wares,"[93] some pieces of which were damaged by careless handling on the long journey south.

Figure 29
From Ohr's appearance (at far left) this photo was taken sometime around 1905. Although the location has been identified as Newcomb College, that is highly unlikely: these are the wrong people, in the wrong setting, doing the wrong things, for it to be Newcomb.

The certificate from the exposition[94] simply read "Silver Medal," but George embellished it a bit, putting a sharp edge on his version when he painted up the inevitable surreal placard: MEDAL, FOR & THE ONLY - INDIVIDUAL - ORIGINAL - ART POTTERY IN THE ST LOUIS EXPOSITION 1904. The weary Biloxian was quite incensed and disappointed. He might just as well toot his own horn, since no one else was going to. In fact no one in the press seems to have noticed very much of what was going on in the dreary mini-world of Mines and Metallurgy, let alone that Ohr had won a silver medal. When the critic Ethel Hutson wrote of the trials of being a potter's wife, recounting the "pitiful story" of

George and St. Louis in her 1905 article "Quaint Biloxi Pottery," she too neglected to mention the silver medal, though George saw to it that his placard was pictured.[95] It seems a cruel irony that Ohr's greatest moment of triumph, capped by the prize that should have brought him fame long overdue, was instead completely unnoticed, instantly overlooked as if it never happened. By contrast trade journals like *Keramic Studio* had no problem remembering almost everyone else who showed up in St. Louis, medals or no.[96]

Sometimes requests for his artware did come to Biloxi, and on those occasions his spirits would rise. Yet George was firm in demanding a high price for his mud babies and that discouraged most dealers. A New York art shop ordered several pieces, but in all these were hard and bitter times. He certainly wasn't forgotten, just unappreciated. The United States Potters' Association wrote to George in 1905 requesting him to send a sampling of his work for a display they were putting together. Their annual convention was subsequently held in the Hotel Raleigh in Washington, D.C. Among the luminaries there were senators and congressmen, along with representatives from most of the leading ceramics manufacturers in the country. The association put up a wonderful exhibit of wares in the hotel, including "a few pieces" from almost every producer. The Blacksmith Potter sent his selection along with his sentiments, which the president of the association quoted in his opening address: "Mr. George E. Ohr, the noted and eccentric potter of Biloxi, Miss., covered the situation in answer to the committee's request for specimens of his goods, when he said: 'I send you four pieces, but it is as easy to pass judgment on my productions from four pieces as it would be to take four lines from Shakespeare and guess the rest.'"[97]

After the convention a large body of fine artwares made by America's premier potteries was offered to the Smithsonian Institution through the Art and Design Committee of the United States Potters' Association. Among these were a group by Ohr, and on March 13, 1906, the United States National Museum accepted a splendid red "small handled vase" 8½ inches tall, returning the remaining pieces, presumably to Biloxi.[98]

BILOXI MISS^N CLAY. ART. WORK.
CANNOT BE DUPLICATED. G. E. OHR. 'FECIT'

Always unpredictable, Mr. Ohr got it into his head around this time that it was finally the right moment to share his work with a wider audience in a sustained presentation. Accordingly he carefully chose fifty specimens that as a group formed a somewhat representative statement of his art and boxed them up in a huge crate. This unsolicited gift he sent to the Delgado Art Museum in New Orleans. The people in charge of the museum were apparently delighted with the bequest and selected twelve pieces from the treasure for their permanent exhibition, explaining by letter that there was simply no room for any more than that in the display cases. "George was furious. All or nothing. 'Send it all back immediately,' he wrote. And in due time, the large crate arrived."[99] It was still standing in his bedroom in Biloxi unopened long after George had died.

It can be inferred that Ohr continued to show his work at fairs and the like for the next few years: a crate of pottery bearing a shipping label indicating that it had returned to Biloxi from something called the Boston Exposition, remained sealed, its contents also hidden for decades.[100] (This entombing instinct was a strange and suggestive gesture, consistent with his almost self-inflicted obscurity—it would emerge again in an even more macabre context.)

Figure 30
The pottery showroom, c. 1905. The poster on the far wall reads "Mobile Mardigras Carnival March 6 & 7 1905." The newspaper headline on the left announces a "Great American Collection of Rare Porcelain," and so underscores Ohr's awareness of what was happening in the world beyond Biloxi.

WORLD'S FAMOUS ART POTTER.
G.E. OHR OF BILOXI MISS." HIS CHALLENGE HAS BEEN STANDING FOR 17 YEARS TO MEET ANY POTTER ON EARTH CREATING SHAPES — TO-DAY HE CHALLENGES ALL TOGETHER

OFFICE OF WORLDS FAIR REGISTER

BOOTHS
FOR LEASE

WANTED
NAMES OF ALL VISITORS

PLEASE LEAVE US YOUR NAME

Figure 31
Figure 31
George in front of an armory (location unknown), soon after having won his silver medal at the St. Louis fair, c. 1905.

Figure 32
Ohr pumping up the fuel tank on his portable kiln. According to the *Clay-worker* (September 1905), this is the St. Louis fair, but it looks more like the backyard of the armory in the previous picture.

clay babies so that a future, more enlightened people might dig them up and understand.

A variety of dated pieces, almost all of them bisque, survive from the years 1902 through 1907. Some of these are wonderful time-caught glimpses of the master's soaring spirit, others simple bowls, small undistinguished vessels, and minor trinkets. Ohr apparently did a good deal of experimenting with different kinds of clay during the period from 1905 to 1907. Several bisque pots exist carrying the designation *Mud from N.O. Street 1905,* and one of them continues, *Potter sed-2-clay = B ware = and it was = a thing of the future Biloxi 6–31–05.* A thing of the future indeed.

One two-inch-tall piece reads *O'1 SI-RR Pier Clay 1906,* and another is inscribed *Channel mud of Biloxi 1906.* An unglazed vegetal form, looking something like an apple with a stem, bears an inscription that is one of the few extant records of a sale: *Mary had a little lamb and George has a little pot·Ohr·E. going, going, gone = and sold to the Mr = WV La Rose, Biloxi Mississippi, Oct. 28, 1906 for 55c.* At least George was in a good humor that day.[102] Yet another vase carries the maverick's latest pseudonym: *Complements from the IT-Pot R 11–5–1906.*[103]

The photographs from this final era also suggest that by some time around 1904 "Biloxies Ohrmer Khayam" had turned his hand primarily to producing extraordinary shapes exclusive of glaze.[104] Though George continued to work, and apparently continued to teach the craft to occasional students, by 1909 his greatest accomplishments were well behind him.

There is also a family tradition that George sent his wares to the Jamestown Ter-Centennial Exposition held from April 26 to November 30 (1907), in Norfolk, Virginia; that too is likely, but uncorroborated.[101]

Unwilling to sell his art for less than its worth, unable to interest either the art world or the nation in purchasing the totality of his creation, Ohr found it easy to hide it, to leave it crated, or worse. One evening he went to Back Bay carrying a shovel, a lantern, and sack full of pottery. As he walked through the dark woods, in a ritual born of utter despair, he buried his

The Master Potter was visited by Della Mc-Leod, whose observations, recounted in an article for the Memphis *Commercial Appeal* (June 27, 1909), are especially significant because they are among the last views we have of the Biloxi Art Pottery Unlimited. "He contends," McLeod reports of George, "that all pottery, when it comes to glazing, owes its beauty to accident. . . . Artists from all parts of the world make pilgrimages to this queer little spider-webbed rookery. But few agree with Ohr in his claim to greatness through originality in shapes.

If he has achieved any special distinction in his work it is in the really beautiful 'accidental' glazes. He has cabinets upon cabinets out in the weather, leaning against the side of his dwelling house, in which are hidden away some wonderful bits of color. There is a case in all shades of blue, one a quivering shade of peacock with bronze shadows showing red lights in the sun, another is a gun-metal bowl that turns to molten gold once the light strikes it, or still another purple pitcher on which the fire has burned withered wisteria petals. He very generously disclaims any credit for the coloring of these and the others equally lovely, explaining that the fire did it." As for Biloxi's "greatest Ohr-na-ment," she says, "the queer genius of the place, George Ohr, [is] a piece of humanity as hard to catalogue as his wares. A pair of eyes like those of some wild wood creature, startled one moment and the next full of the baleful glow of hatred for a world that denies him the place to which he knows he has a claim."[105]

In the fall of 1909 George got into a bit of a disagreement with the city fathers: Biloxi had failed to complete a drainage project in a timely fashion and Ohr, out of patience with their dawdling, dug his own ditch and wound up in the slammer. The photograph (Figure 34) shows George "under bond" next to his nameless "Jail Chum" who seems to be pausing from his labors repairing the street—it was common practice in the South at the time to use "convict labor" in the public service. The Mad Potter had a sense of history, both past and yet to come, and so he brought a photographer to carefully document his travail, that we might properly empathize.

The Ohr family, no doubt instigated by its oldest son Leo, had tried to persuade the potter to have a sale and get rid of all his pots and debts at once, but George would have none of it. Still, he was turning fifty-three and weary of the struggle that seemed hopelessly lost. He had cast himself as Sleeping Beauty and now, out of patience, worn thin, and tired from all the demands that a lack of respect invites, he was ready for a new game, ready to give up his shop to his sons who would make better use of it. They assured him of that. Besides, he was getting on in years and his health wasn't what it

used to be. George could not possibly sell his life cheap, but he could crate it, killed babies and all, and put it away quietly in a dark corner, safe.

When the census man asked his occupation in April 1910, George answered "Art Potter—own shop." By then both Leo and Lio were chauffeurs, and Portman was a lighthouse keeper. Leo at nineteen was an up-and-coming fast mover, Biloxi's first automobile mechanic. He

Figure 33
The Mad Potter with a wonderful selection of his art ware. The display may be inside the armory pictured in the two previous figures, c. 1905.

Figure 34
The sign tells it all: "G.E. Ohr under bond for upholding the law of Mississippi and my jail chum of Biloxi Sept. 6/09."

ran the Coast's premier jitney, busing folks between Biloxi and Point Cadet. At $2.50 an hour a courageous tourist could take a hair-raising ride in a one-cylinder Cadillac owned by the Biloxi Machine Works and driven by Leo E. Ohr. It wasn't long before he had the fastest power boat in the South as well—Leo was a modern man in a hurry.

They tore down the old pagoda tower—no one needed to see it anymore. They ripped off the porch—with the pots boxed up it didn't seem to matter. They cut a gaping hole in the face of the building so the cars could drive in, took up the signs, and made it all look so different. With OHR BOYS AUTO REPAIRING SHOP painted across the top, Biloxi's first garage opened around 1910. Most of the ten thousand mud babies were laid unwrapped in large, open wooden crates. Dozens to a box, haphazardly placed one on top of another, they were pushed away in the third-floor attic.[106] The once and wonderful Biloxi Art Pottery Unlimited vanished forever. [107]

With time heavy on his hands, George got into all sorts of mischief. [108] His father died on July 8, 1904, and his mother not long after on December 28, 1905. He and Josephine, who tenderly took care of them both in their last years, inherited some money and a good bit of real estate. Always naive, Ohr later sold a plot of that land at much below the actual value,

and when the shrewd buyer promptly resold it for a handsome profit George was irate. He ranted and picketed and yelled, making a public nuisance of himself until he was finally arrested. That was in 1910. Oh, how the world conspired to prove him inadequate. [109]

The Biloxi M.D. loved to dress up and get out of himself; he never missed a carnival or Mardi Gras where he might masquerade. One year he wore a long robe and wandered the streets as Father Time, scythe and all, mumbling prophesy and gathering crowds. He had let his long, white beard grow full and shaggy, a perfect sight. Now venomous from the land debacle, Ohr built himself a Mardi Gras float. Flanked by effigies of the villains who had done him wrong, saintly George, wearing a white, flowing gown and carrying a monumental cross, was hauled up and back the streets of Biloxi. The fact that he had long been an agnostic only added to the performance. [110] Mr. Ohr had produced a "happening" with philosophical and political overtones, a quixotic bit of protest street theater, but most onlookers were simply appalled; the old madman had outdone himself. [111]

However, far from the fire, the IT-Pot R had not lost his love of the wheel nor forgotten his craft; Around this time Ohr taught Manuel Jalanovich to work the wheel.[112] And he had great plans for "Putting Potters Wheels in to School houses – of four towns on this Coast— and Give me [Ohr] A chance to teach – A thousand (more or less) how to make POTS— Pots, All kinds of Pottery pots—And make Harrison County the Center and Stamping Grounds of the *entire U.S.A.*"[113]

With his long, white beard and hair, George looked older than he was in those last years. He had been a heavy cigarette smoker for a long time, and his penultimate child, still young enough to do the family fetching, remembers the frequent prodding—"Ojo, get me Piedmonts"—a nickel would buy ten. There's even a picture of George with a cigar jutting from his mouth, one of those old photos that Josie kept in a cardboard box with her letters, long after he was gone. But in 1915 he was still feisty and railing as ever in a stream-of-consciousness torrent, this time against machine-made art:

Figure 35
The Ohr Boys Auto Repairing Shop. That's Leo at the left filling the radiator of the 1903 Cadillac and Josephine standing near George, who is astride a motorcycle. It looks like autumn, perhaps around 1910.

Figure 36
The Mad Potter carrying a cross on his infamous Mardi Gras float, here parked in front of the family garage.

"No real Art Pottery is now CREATED on this Old Dirt Daubers Ball— While the Brush and Chisle Artist Still Domineers on Earth as of yore....We are living in an Age of Wheels – more wheels, and wheels within Wheels—And MACHINE ART Works – is A fake and Fraud of the deepest die"[114]

George was far from reconciled with the irony that the mass-produced wares of the major potteries were widely accepted as art, despite the fact that they were made by several people working independently on a production line. By contrast there was no doubt who sired his mud babies.

G.E. Ohr Will and can Make any of the high Priced Payers — of Rookwood Teco —Vanbriggle or Capitalized Companies Servents Work— "show their HAND—As to where is the Potter-that can" "Father the Art Produced—The outcome would "BE" that Five - or Fifteen Did the "JOB on Pot While in Sculpertng— Carving - of Paintings - it Dont Take A Doz' to Accomplish Art Pottery—(Originality does not Emenate from A Company or regiment ((Cromos and Photos Are "PICTURES" — But sutch dont command Fabulous Prices As "Real — head — heart - hand - and Soul ""ART.""[115]

George's philosophy was the apotheosis of the Arts and Crafts spirit before it made truce with the machine, closed its eyes, and lost its nerve. Only the Mud Dauber wouldn't compromise, and his babies were in the dark.[116]

Ohr was a potter who saw himself as an artist (and he was both). He loved the wheel, and the work that sprang from it was firmly grounded in the traditions of pottery. However bizarre and wonderful the shapes, Ohr forced on them a topology that spun off the wheel. Yet the vessel was less, for its function was subsumed as it became more the idiom of his art: the pot was the very medium in which he plied that art. Ohr's whole life as America's premier artist-potter[117] had been spent in the pursuit of a "Real—head—heart – hand – and Soul ""ART.""

The pains in his throat, the coughing, he must have known what it was—he had already been suffering for years and was seeing a doctor in New Orleans. That's where they assumed he was going when he left the house on December 31, 1917. Strangely enough, no one went with

39

Figure 37
George E. Ohr during the last years of his life.

him, as if they had no idea of how ill he really was. A week or so later, having completely vanished, George sent a letter to his doctor postmarked Chicago; perhaps he went there to confirm the diagnosis of cancer. "Our understanding," Leo told the newspaper reporter, "was that he was going to New Orleans to go into a hospital for treatment. He did not communicate with us after he left and we do not understand why he has not done so." In any event, old George, who was older than he should have been, was adrift again; all alone as he had been when he rode a barge with the first load of clay down the Tchoutacabouffa River, just a moment before. "When I am gone," he once said,

"my work will be praised, honored, and cherished. It will come."[118] He had indeed created real, head, heart, hand, and soul art, and he knew it. "He was a wise man the Good Lord sent down here to make stuff and show the world."[119] On a Sunday morning in Biloxi, April 7, 1918, at 3:10, with his mud babies buried silent in their crates, George Edgar Ohr died.[120]

Old-timers remembered him, perennial child that he was, hard riding his motorcycle. Roaring down the beach, moustache wrapped around his ears, his long white beard flying in the breeze, and those eyes, those wild eyes.

Plate 1   Tall handled vase, c. 1895–1900. Height: 11¾ inches. Private collection, New York.

Plate 2
Vase, c. 1890
Height: 9⅞ inches. Private collection, New York.

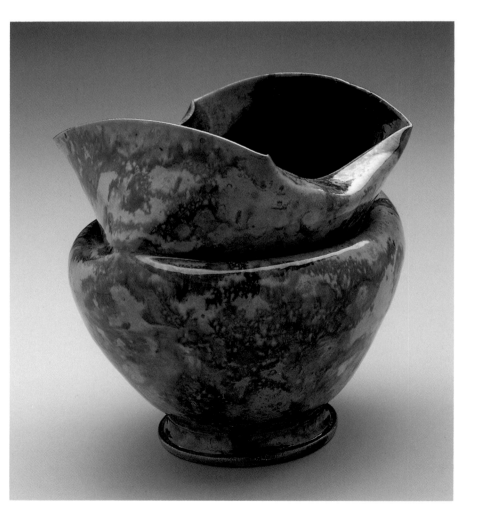

Plate 3
Vase, c. 1895–1900.
Height: 5½ inches. Private collection, New York.

Plate 4   Double-handled vase, c. 1898. Height: 5¾ inches. Charles Cowles, New York City.

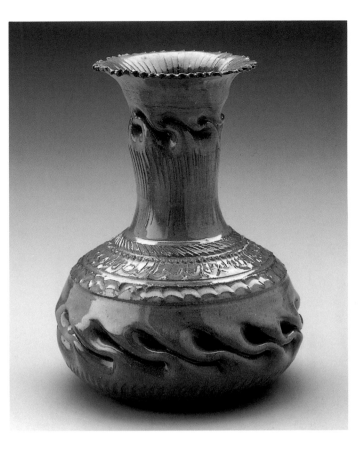

Plate 5
Vase, c. 1895–1900. Height: 4¾ inches.
Private collection, New York.

Plate 6
Handled vase, c. 1898–1907.
Height: 10½ inches. Private collection,
New York.

Plate 7   Handled vase, c. 1895–1900. Height: 8¼ inches. Barbara and Jack Hertog, New York City.

Plate 8   Handled vase, c. 1895–1900. Height 8⅞ inches. Private collection, New York City.

Plate 9
Tall handled vase, c. 1895–1900.
Height: 10¾ inches. Private collection,
New York.

Plate 10
Tall handled vase, 1894. Height: 14½ inches.
Private collection, New York.

Plate 11   Handled vase, c. 1895–1900. Height: 10½ inches. Private collection, New York.

Plate 12
Vase, c. 1895–1900.
Height: 6¾ inches. Tom Dillenberg and Judy
Espinar, New York City.

Plate 13
Handled vase, c. 1895–1900.
Height: 10½ inches. Private collection,
Montague, New Jersey.

Plate 14
Snake-handled cup, c. 1895–1900.
Height: 3¾ inches. Private
collection, New York.

Plate 15
Vase, 1895. Height: 8⅜ inches.
Private collection, New York.

Plate 16   Tall sectioned vase, 1899. Height: 16 inches. Private collection, New York.

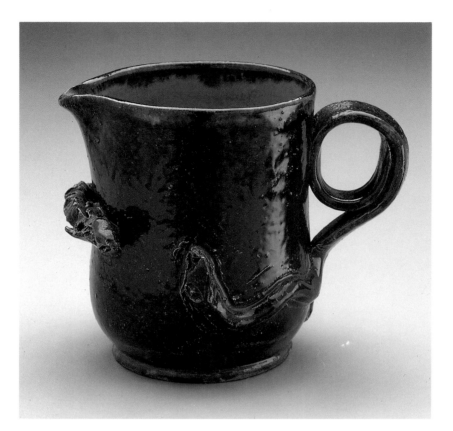

Plate 17
Small pitcher, c. 1895–1900.
Height: 3½ inches. Private
collection, New York.

Plate 18
Pitcher, c. 1898–1907.
Height: 8½ inches. Private
collection, New York.

Plate 19   Winged vase, c. 1895–1900. Height: 13 inches. Betty and Robert Hut, New York City.

Plate 20
Vase, c. 1895–1900.
Height: 5¾ inches. Private collection,
New York City.

Plate 21
Vase, c. 1895–1900. Height: 7 inches.
Private collection, New York.

54

Plate 22   Pitcher, c. 1895–1900. Height: 8½ inches. Private collection, New York.

Plate 24
Footed vase, c. 1895–1900.
Height: 8⅜ inches. Private collection,
New York City.

Plate 23
Tall vase, c. 1895–1900.
Height: 12⅜ inches. Private collection,
New York.

Plate 25
Tall footed vase, c. 1895–1900.
Height: 12⅞ inches. Private
collection, New York City.

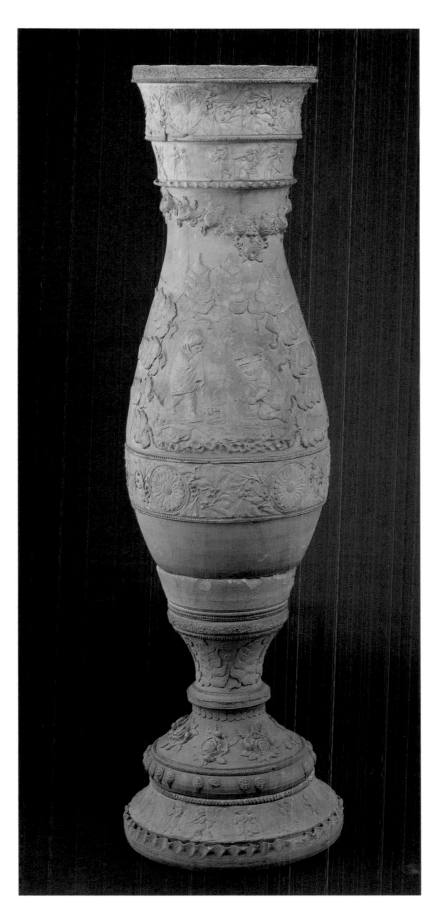

Plate 26   Monumental vase, c. 1892. Height: 61½ inches. Private collection, New York.

Plate 28
Vase, c. 1895–1900.
Height: 6⅝ inches. Martin Eidelberg,
New York City.

Plate 27
Vase, c. 1895–1900. Height: 6¼ inches.
Private collection, New York City.

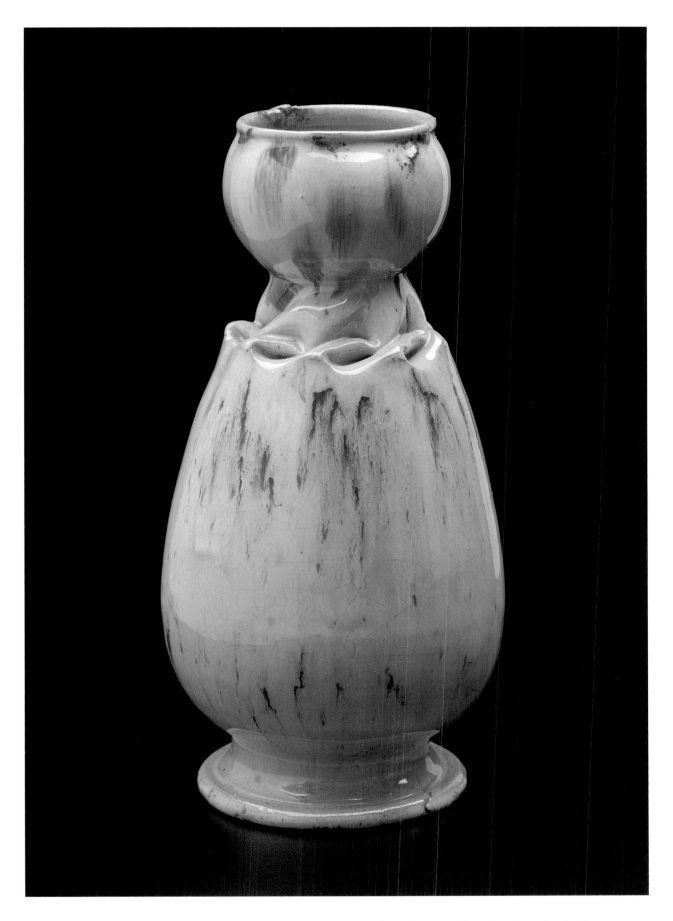

Plate 29   Footed vase, c. 1895–1900. Height: 7⅜ inches. Private collection, New York City.

Plate 30   Small bowl, c. 1895–1900. Height: 4 inches. Private collection, New York.

Plate 31   Small bowl, c. 1895–1900. Height: 3½ inches. Private collection, New York.

Plate 32
Small bowl, c. 1903.
Height: 3⅛ inches.
Private collection, New York.

Plate 33
Vase, c. 1898–1907.
Height: 4 inches. Private collection,
Montague, New Jersey.

Plate 34   Tall vase, c. 1895–1900. Height: 17 inches. Bonnie and James Udell, New York City.

Plate 35   Composite form, c. 1900. Height: 8⅜ inches. Private collection, New York.

After hearing secondhand rumors about eccentric pottery, imagine yourself in the position of Lyle Saxon, a writer who walked into George Ohr's storeroom, not knowing what to expect, four years after Ohr's death in 1918. I will let Saxon's words evoke the breadth, the strangeness, the uniqueness of Ohr's ceramic work:

the shutters of the window are. . .partly ajar. . . .Within are. . .shelves filled with rows of pottery, dull and lustrous; some of the pieces are almost classic in their chaste simplicity, while others are grotesque and distorted, wilfully misshapen. . . .You pause and stand looking at the vessels displayed there. . .arrested by their beauty, intrigued by their strangeness. For never have you seen craftsmanship which bore the mark of the maker to such a degree. . . . [C]ross[ing] the threshold. . .[y]ou find yourself in a room which is filled from end to end with pottery; it stands upon the shelves, upon the floor, in the window sills; tables are covered with it, and, as you look through the door of the adjoining room, you see other pieces. . . jumbled together in confusion—a veritable museum of spheres, globes and rhomboids as well as pieces of irregular shapes which you cannot name. . . .There is something almost uncanny in the room. . . .you are amazed to see how strongly the potter has marked these pieces of clay with his own strange personality . . . .what a genius [he has] for the grotesque. . . [the] fantastic. . .[and the] weird.

You are holding a. . .teapot, a beautifully conceived and executed design, simple and lovely in line. The potter is a master—and yet. . .you are almost shocked at the ungainliness of the piece next to it, an unwieldy jar, top-heavy, fantastically, comically ugly with three handles, all placed awry, as if with malicious intent. A veritable monster of a pot. Perverse, but humorous, too. . . .You can almost hear the potter's chuckle as he turned it on the potter's wheel. A slap in the face of conventional art—futuristic! The potter. . .has tired of the beautiful, and finds joy in the bizarre, the ugly. . . .Suddenly, you find yourself liking the potter immensely. You can imagine his personality; genial, yet canny and wise; a master of his art, yet a joker.

Ah, here is a man who can laugh at life. . . . you feel that you know the potter. . .for here is bare stark personality in every jar and jug.[1]

Saxon's description of his encounter with Ohr's work conveys a vivid sense of the Mississippi potter's idiosyncratic genius, a genius that has only begun to be recognized over the last fifteen years. During the time that Ohr was creating his most radical works, most members of the contemporary art pottery movement were painting floral motifs on largely standardized shapes, although a few adventurous souls were

"No Two Alike": The Triumph of Individuality

BY ROBERT A. ELLISON, JR.

Figure 38
Watercolor portrait of G. E. Ohr, c. 1890, by William Woodward. Jordan Lubitz and Eugene Hecht, New York.

The radical nature of Ohr's work did not spring spontaneously from the Mississippi mud but evolved out of humble beginnings. Around 1879 or 1880, after many diverse and frustrating jobs, he received an offer from a potter of functional ware named Joseph Meyer to come to New Orleans as his apprentice. Ohr leapt at the offer, perhaps without knowing that those were auspicious years for entering the field of ceramics. Although his provincial apprenticeship taught him only the rudiments of making useful pottery, he was immediately enchanted by the magic of the potter's wheel. Not only could he earn a living, he had also found his element: "When I found the potter's wheel I felt it all over like a wild duck in water," Ohr declared.[4] With the zeal of a convert, he set out to learn all about ceramics, absorbing examples from folk potters, industry, ceramic history, and the developing art pottery movement.

Figures 39–40
Ohr's functional wares: above, pieces salvaged from Ohr's studio after it was destroyed by the Biloxi fire in 1894; below, storage jar. Except for very basic pieces, Ohr could not resist adding little decorative flourishes such as the concentric throwing marks and the slight metallic sheen to the glaze on this second piece. Private collection, New York.

making symmetrical vessels on the potter's wheel. Ohr's bizarre forms presented an abstract sort of three-dimensional decoration based on manipulating the form of the vessel itself. This approach dramatically broadened the possibilities for ceramic form, heretofore tied to the symmetry of the potter's wheel, and set Ohr apart from all other potters of the period, whether European or American, thereby thrusting his work into unknown aesthetic territory. "I have a notion . . . that I am a mistake—misfit."[2] Ohr once remarked, and later described his sense of being an outsider by explaining, "Suppose 5 hen eggs were put under a brood and somebody somewhere made a mistake and got a duck egg in the job lot, that duck is going to be in some very hot aqua."[3] Indeed so great was his artistic isolation that not until some forty-five years after his retirement in 1910 was the aesthetic viability of manipulating wheel-thrown vessels rediscovered by ceramic artists.

For a number of years Ohr's work consisted only of functional and souvenir wares somewhat like the work of the American folk potters, wares he continued to make throughout his career and that enabled him to stay afloat. Even in 1909 he was still selling basic, useful pieces to the local population[5] — flowerpots, water coolers, brown jugs, cups, saucers, chimney flues, storage crocks, teapots, mugs, pitchers, bowls, harvest jugs, jars, hanging planters, and garden urns (Figures 39, 40). This explains the occasional heavy, dull, simply glazed, functional vessel that turns up among his later delicate, artistic work.

Ohr's outrageous improvisations were the result of an eccentric and profoundly original imagination obsessed with creating unique forms for each ceramic vessel. The Biloxi potter transformed an eclectic variety of sources into strange works with only subtle evidence of influences and affinities. Ultimately, his quest drove him to lay his hands on his perfect wheel-thrown vessels and to manipulate them into unprecedented shapes.

Figures 41–42
Opposite page, examples of Ohr's souvenir ware: top, artist's palette with bowl and pitcher and, below, miniature chamber pot with ceramic feces. Private collection, New York City.

After his introduction to ceramics, Ohr quickly achieved a basic proficiency on the potter's wheel. However instead of settling in and selling his wares he immediately set out to expand his horizons beyond that of the provincial potter. "After knowing how to boss a little piece of clay into a gallon jug," he recalled, "I pulled out of New Orleans and took a zigzag trip for 2 years, and got as far as Dubuque, Milwaukee, Albany, down the Hudson, and zigzag back home. I sized up every potter and pottery in 16 states, and never missed a show window, illustration or literary dab on ceramics since that time, 1881."[6] Given his need to earn a living, he probably worked his way around the country using either his newfound potter's skill or his numerous other skills.

Aside from this sketchy itinerary, Ohr left us no other clues as to what he did or saw on his ambitious, two-year odyssey, but an analysis of the probable path of his trip and the potters and resources he may have encountered suggests certain influences and precedents that are indeed borne out in Ohr's functional, souvenir, and even artistic work. On his journey Ohr probably sought out those potters who worked in the folk and utilitarian earthenware and stoneware tradition, craftspeople who were struggling to hold out against the inevitable industrial tidal wave that was engulfing the country. Crocks, jugs, and flowerpots continued to be handmade during these years, but industry was taking over more and more of the tableware and kitchenware market with mass-produced ironstone ceramics and metal products. Potters frequently made souvenir and decorative ware to broaden their markets.

If Ohr gave his itinerary in its chronological order, we could assume that he traveled by Mississippi riverboat from New Orleans to Dubuque. If this is true, then as it moved up the Mississippi his boat passed within ten miles of Anna, Illinois, home of the Kirkpatrick stoneware pottery, which was in operation from 1859 to 1896. The two Kirkpatrick brothers competed against industrial production with standardized but hand-thrown storage vessels and other utilitarian products. As a sideline they created an inventive range of hand-modeled souvenir ware: jugs embellished with snakes and figures, toby-like figural pitchers, pig flasks with incised railroad maps, miniature jugs, pioneer log cabins, and mugs incised with poems or inscriptions.[7] This sort of work occasionally turns up in Ohr's souvenir pieces: indeed an Ohr pig flask dated 1882 (Figure 43) is made of stoneware, glazed with an Albany slip, and carries a clever inscription, all of which are characteristic of the work at Anna. But the competitive and inventive Ohr added a detail to his pig not found in the Anna prototypes, partitioning the pig into two sections and inscribing "rye" in the tail section and "gin" in the head section. The date of the piece corresponds to the time of Ohr's trip, so it is highly probable

that he made it at the Kirkpatricks' workshop. Further evidence rests on the fact that the pig was not in Ohr's estate, but was recently purchased in Illinois' neighboring state, Iowa.

Like the Kirkpatricks, Ohr occasionally applied reptiles to his vessels, although they were much more rudimentary and schematic, and made log cabins, mugs with inscriptions, and various pieces with poems impressed into the surface. But throughout his career Ohr's production included brown jugs, miniature chamber pots holding ceramic feces, leopard and donkey heads, crabs, potatoes, apples, puzzle mugs, shells, cannons, books, wicker boxes, artists' palettes, miniature spittoons, hats, and a large variety of banks and inkwells (Figures 41, 42, 94, 111). He sold this type of

Figure 43
Pig flask by Ohr dated "Mch 25 1882." The flask is incised with the words, "Mr. Murphy dont drink, but Allways keep a little good old rye for His Friends in this Hog's [hand pointing to rear end]." On the other side is incised the advice, "Suck this Hogs Nose for Gin." Tony and Marie Shank, Marion, South Carolina.

ware to the Northerners who came to Biloxi in the winter and to the visitors from the Gulf Coast who came in the summer.

The significant difference between Ohr and the Kirkpatricks is that souvenir ware was the primary creative effort of the Anna potters. While they also pursued an interest in social and political symbolism (e.g., the temperance movement), they expressed it through naive attempts at realism that frequently resulted in a folk art type of caricature. For Ohr, on the other hand, souvenir ware was a minor aspect of his work, and he mainly focused his energies on pieces of a more abstract, artistic nature. "These souvenirs, it must be understood, are not considered pottery proper," one observer reported after an interview with Ohr. "It is from the sale of them, however, that the pot in the Ohr kitchen continues to boil."[8] Although he assigned a secondary status to his souvenir ware, it does have charm and inventiveness, and much of it displays the same careful attention to craftsmanship and glazing that his art pottery does. In contrast to his artistic work, however, ready precedents for these pieces existed in commercial trinkets and souvenirs made of ceramics, metal, and glass, and in the whimsies of the glassmakers and folk potters.

Continuing his zigzag back home, Ohr would have found a lively, viable earthenware tradition still surviving in central Pennsylvania and the Shenandoah Valley. All the skills of the potter were being practiced there and a variety of imaginative shapes were created ranging from simple, useful ware to puzzle mugs, hanging planters, wall pockets, vases with scalloped necks, and flowerpots with ruffled rims. In addition there were hand-modeled figurines and animals as well as the log cabins, potato bottles, and banks of all descriptions, which Ohr also made.

In Pennslyvania, Ohr might have seen a particular style of fancy, commemorative flowerpot from Chester County, frequently inscribed and dated from the 1820s (compare Figures 47 and 48). The characteristic features of the pots and their saucers were deep and richly ruffled rims in single and double rows, a decorative device that Ohr appropriated and applied to his artistic wares. In extreme examples he applied multiple rows of ruffles over the whole vase. The teapots of Thomas Haig of Philadelphia from the 1820–30s also must have impressed Ohr with their distinctively undulating profiles glazed in black or brown (Figure 46).

In the Shenandoah Valley, our itinerant potter would have found the ceramic work of the late John and Solomon Bell, brothers whose separate operations were being continued by their sons. The Bells had made basic functional ware, art ware with applied decorations, folk sculpture, molded pitchers decorated with scenes in low relief, and some gently manipulated vases (Figure 49). Though crude in execution, their art pottery exuded vitality. In their attempt to stay afloat in the face of industrial competition, however, the Bells, like other folk potters, were forced to fill the roles of functional and souvenir potter and to carve out a niche for a heavy-handed, country-style art pottery—a path Ohr also followed, albeit with highly sophisticated art pottery.

The most intriguing example of this late-nineteenth-century country art pottery that Ohr may have seen was that of Anthony Baecher, active in Winchester, Virginia, in his later years until his death in 1889 (Figure 50). Baecher's style frequently featured excessive amounts of artistic detail. A typical vase, for example, has a long neck with a swelling body, looping handles, and a clutter of heavy applied decoration. Although their decoration is representational, his vases bear strong resemblance to the Ohr vase we see in Figure 51 or to others with looping handles, twisting, and ruffling. If Baecher's work was not the prototype for this aspect of Ohr's work, it certainly would have been a lesson for Ohr in visual complexity.

In contrast to the wares of the folk potters, with their limited production and local distribution, industrial ceramics were present everywhere. Ohr may well have been impressed by certain highly refined industrial wares such as the Belleek line initiated by Ott & Brewer of Trenton, New Jersey, in 1882. While Belleek featured painted decoration, Ohr may have noticed the frequent indenting of the bodies and the ruffling and asymmetry of the necks (Figure 52). This ware's eggshell-thin porcelain body, achieved through a careful process of molding, may have challenged Ohr to equal such thinness using the much more difficult technique of the potter's wheel.

Given his penchant for individuality, industrially made ceramics might seem like an implausible source of inspiration for Ohr. On the whole, however, his attitude toward the concepts and techniques of industrial production was somewhat contradictory. On the one hand, he revered the idea of creating unique pieces. "The human does not live or ever will live or ever B born & hope to duplicate my Twisted shapes," he remarked, "make 'em that way on purpose, and could not do it 'over' myself."[9] He also feared industry's propensity to produce cheap copies of any work that became fashionable. Yet Ohr himself made an earthenware imitation of a glass copy of a Chinese "peach blow" porcelain vase, the original of which had made headlines in 1886 by selling for $18,000.[10] Ohr's contradictory attitude is also confirmed by the molds he made from glass pitchers and paperweights, English ceramic pitchers, and found objects such as seashells and crabs.[11] In spite of his obsession with creating variety in his work, he also designed several molds of his own for

pitchers, which frequently portrayed local scenes and were modeled in low relief in a rather crude but charming manner.

These designs for molded pitchers were very much in a nineteenth-century American industrial tradition that began with D. & J. Henderson around 1830. It was continued at midcentury by Norton & Fenton, the Salamander Works (compare Figures 53 and 54), E. & W. Bennett, the American Pottery Company, the United States Pottery Company, and in the last part of the nineteenth century by the workshops of both John and Solomon Bell. But molding was never used by Ohr in his artistic pieces and remains a very minor aspect of his work.

During the 1880s and into the early 1890s, industrially produced glassware exhibited certain fluid Victorian details, and it seems likely that the infectious spirit behind these characteristic details was also picked up by such ceramic makers as Ott & Brewer and George Ohr, and, if only occasionally, by Rookwood Pottery. On the whole, glassmakers appear to have been more interested in color and decoration than in form, and vases and bowls were for the most part of conventional shapes. A range of details

Figures 47–48
Left, fancy ruffled earthenware flowerpot from Chester County, Pennsylvania, probably by the James Pottery, dated 1824. Above, Ohr vase, c. 1895–1900. Early in his career Ohr picked up from the folk potters the device of ruffling the rims of vessels. James: The Metropolitan Museum of Art, New York; Purchase, Virginia Groomes, gift in memory of Mary W. Groomes, 1974. Ohr: Private collection, New York City.

Figure 49
Earthenware vase attributed to Bell Potteries of Strasburg, Virginia, c. 1880. Private collection, New York City.

Figures 50–51
Top, vase by Anthony Baecher of
Winchester, Virginia, c. 1870–89,
compared with a similar piece by Ohr,
below, c. 1898–1907. Baecher:
The Metropolitan Museum of Art,
New York; Sansbury-Mills Fund, 1979.
Ohr: Martin Eidelberg, New York City.

was sometimes added to their necks or rims,
however, including ruffling, indenting, multiple
lobing, and folding into trefoils and quatrefoils.
While glass baskets showed an occasional touch
of free-form asymmetry, which nevertheless
was constrained by feet and handles, generally
glassmakers did not experiment with the total
form of the vessel until Louis Comfort Tiffany
did so in the mid-1890s. But Tiffany developed
only a few forms that can be compared with
Ohr's mature experiments during the same
period.

While Ohr absorbed influences from contemporary craft and industry, he also seems to have
sought out a broad spectrum of historical sources during his trip around 1880–82. During
these years a variety of museums had begun to
spring up in this country. While the Wadsworth
Atheneum in Hartford, Connecticut, and the
Smithsonian Institution in Washington, D. C.,
were founded in the 1840s, the flowering of
American museums began in earnest in the
1870s. The Metropolitan Museum of Art in
New York City was founded in 1870 and displayed a wide range of ceramics by 1875, featuring pieces from Europe, the Mediterranean,
the Orient, and America. From this country
there were examples of redware, Tucker porcelain from Philadelphia, and molded earthenware from the American Pottery Company of
Jersey City, New Jersey, and from the United
States Pottery Company of Bennington, Ver-
mont.[12] The Boston Museum of Fine Arts was
also founded in 1870, followed by the Philadelphia Museum in 1876, the St. Louis Museum in
1879, the Rhode Island School of Design
(which set aside three rooms for an industrial
arts museum) in 1879, the Cincinnati Museum
in 1881, and next year the Corcoran Gallery
in Washington, D. C., and the Art Institute of
Chicago.

Clearly there were opportunities for Ohr to
gain a broad firsthand knowledge of the history
of ceramics in the 1880s and in subsequent
years, and it seems that he did. Such common,
stereotyped forms as the bud-vase (Plates
81,109) and the ewer (Plate 55), for example,
were reinvented to suit his own eccentric fancy.
Ceramic history is vast, however, and only a few
furtive references to historical forms appear in

Ohr's work. One suspects that he appropriated
more than is readily apparent, but that his own
idiosyncratic interpretation so thoroughly
transformed the original source that it became
unrecognizable.

A survey of Ohr's shapes nevertheless reveals a
few traces of foreign historical influence. The
four-thousand-year-history of Chinese ceramics offers a rich heritage of forms, glazes, and
painting, a heritage that was discovered by
American and European potters mainly in the
last quarter of the nineteenth century. Unlike
many potters who based their whole repertoire
of forms on Chinese shapes, Ohr appears to
have found inspiration in only a few. He responded to certain vase forms, one with an
elegant profile (compare Figures 55 and 56),
another of squat form with a multiply lobed
neck (compare Figures 57 and 58). More
obvious was Ohr's fascination with the
cadogan vessel concept (compare Figure 59 and
Plate 128), a teapotlike container with a fixed
lid that is filled through the bottom.[13] This
concept had been used in China since at least
the twelfth century, and later became popular
in Europe; a Chinese example has been in the
Metropolitan Museum of Art in New York City
since 1875. Undoubtedly the trick aspect of
this form appealed to Ohr, and dovetailed with
his interest in constructing another form with a
different trick: puzzle mugs with interconnecting
holes and spouts, which required holding a
finger over the correct hole to prevent spilling
when drinking or pouring. This trick aspect
was used by early European and English potters
on the jug form, although Ohr applied it
mainly to mugs.

Although ancient Greek potters were preoccu-
pied with painted decoration and used only a
limited number of shapes, Ohr did appropriate
at least two of their forms from the fifth century
B.C., one called *Lekythos* (Figure 63) and the
other *Loutrophoros* (Figure 60). Surely he was
also aware of Italian *maiolica* from the six-
teenth century—an Ohr pitcher dated 1886
(Figure 64) bears a striking resemblance to
certain wet-drug jars, both featuring similar
shapes and distinctive spouts emanating from
serpent mouths. In addition he probably
appropriated an elegant globular teapot shape

with pure profile and serpentine spout (Plate 123) from the functional forms produced by the Staffordshire potters of eighteenth-century England.

Ohr was definitely aware of the sixteenth-century French potter Bernard Palissy. Although Ohr applied schematic snakes and reptiles to some of his vessels, his identification was not necessarily with Palissy's life-like representations of reptiles and sea creatures, but more likely with the dramatic story of his trials and sacrifices in search of certain colors for his pottery. Allegedly, Palissy burned his furniture to fire his kiln. It was reported that: "He [Ohr] claims that what Palissy has accomplished in color the world will one day concede he [Ohr] has surpassed in shape."[14]

After his two-year journey, Ohr settled down to serious work. Only two years later, however, a major exhibition was held in the region—the New Orleans Cotton Centennial Exhibition. Although there are no records to confirm the fact, Ohr reported that he exhibited his wares at the 1884–85 fair. A bronze medal does confirm the successful participation of the Linthorpe Pottery of Middlesborough, England,[15] whose work Ohr most probably saw there. Linthorpe's ware in its initial phase, 1879 through 1882, was molded from the designs of the noted industrial designer and theoretician of the decorative arts, Christopher Dresser, and at the New Orleans exhibition Linthorpe's production was still coasting on Dresser's unusual designs. However surprising it might seem that molded ceramics might influence a future art potter, certain aspects of Dresser's work were visually enlightening, for Dresser had a far-ranging mind that assimilated many diverse, exotic styles: Persian, Egyptian, Peruvian, and especially Japanese. In certain cases, Dresser's exoticism resulted in crinkling, indenting, twisting, and asymmetry (Figures 65, 67), shapes perhaps inspired by the various gourd forms found in Japanese ceramics. These works were surely Ohr's first exposure to truly unconventional shapes. Dresser's work with three-dimensional forms emphasized that beauty could be achieved through the structure of an object rather than applied ornamentation, an influential concept that would come to be applied in different ways, from the art nouveau with its organic structures to modernism with its severe functional form.

Salted among the odd Dresser shapes for Linthorpe were some pure and simple vessels decorated solely with glaze. Around 1880, this concept was as progressive as that of integrating ornament with structure, for Victorian aesthetics dictated that ornamentation was necessary for a work to be considered artistic. Only through the influence of Oriental ceramics in

Figure 52
Ott & Brewer's porcelain Belleek ware, c. 1890, Trenton, New Jersey. The Metropolitan Museum of Art, New York; Purchase, Edgar J. Kaufmann Charitable Foundation, 1968.

Figures 53–54
Examples of molded functional ware— far left, pitcher by Salamander Works, New York City, c. 1850; left, Ohr pitcher depicting paddle-wheeler, c. 1893–1906. Salamander: Private collection, New York City. Ohr: Brooklyn Museum; Dick S. Ramsay Fund.

Figures 55–56
Above, Chinese Sung dynasty vase, 960–1280, compared with an Ohr vase at right from c. 1895–1900. Sung vase: The Metropolitan Museum of Art, New York; Rogers Fund, 1939. Ohr: Private collection, New York City.

the latter part of the nineteenth century was the West exposed to the idea that simple forms simply glazed could have aesthetic merit on their own. Although Ohr is most widely known for his formally radical pieces, he too seems to have been influenced by the purity frequently found in Oriental ceramics, perhaps through Dresser's work. Pure form and glaze remained a small but consistent portion of his artistic output.

As a designer, Dresser was a product of an aesthetic renewal that took place in the second half of the nineteenth century, one that prompted reappraisals in all the decorative arts. These reappraisals, whether American or European, owed a debt to the philosophies that had emanated from the English design reform movement of midcentury. Enlightened Englishmen had been appalled by how rapidly the Industrial Revolution had eliminated the craftsman and co-opted all areas of taste, design, and production techniques. Inappropriate use of materials, the expediency of copying historical styles, and

thoughtless mass production featuring excessive amounts of applied ornament that obscured function and disguised construction were the leading anathemas for the reformers.

Although sober, rational, scientifically oriented English minds turned away from the decorative historicism that so insistently characterized nineteenth-century design, certain propositions deriving from Gothic construction and medieval craft came to play important roles in the design reform movement.[16] Principles such as the appropriate use of materials, straightforward construction, and an emphasis on handiwork served as basic guideposts; it was thought that all the features of a design should have a purpose and that ornament should only be used to enhance the essential construction;[17] applied ornament came under attack for not being in keeping with the Gothic spirit. Starting as early as 1837 special art schools were established to train designers, who were to collaborate with industry, to elevate the quality of their products. Christopher Dresser, who was educated in this system, exemplified a new breed of designer who, it was hoped, would create personal styles connected with contemporary life to replace the mindless use of historical styles. As far as subject matter, nature, especially plants and flowers, seemed particularly close to the hearts of a population that was increasingly alienated by widespread industrialization.

At a certain point a less rational, more spiritual note was injected into the debate by John Ruskin's passionate love for the variations created by "the hand of the maker," and his violent hatred of the machine, its products, and its effects on the workers. Ruskin's focus on the context of how an object was created produced an offshoot of the design reform movement that attempted to roll back the Industrial Revolution and remove the steps between design and execution by eliminating the division of labor. This would reunite the roles of artist and worker in one person, once again combining art and life, as was the case in the Middle Ages. The leading proponent of Ruskin's philosophy and one who exemplified it in both word and deed was William Morris. In addition to having worked as an artist-craftsman, Morris lectured and wrote widely on behalf of the "lesser" arts.

Design reform ideas were already permeating America when the Philadelphia Centennial Exhibition opened in 1876. This fair introduced designs from exotic cultures around the world as well as the latest trends from England and Europe to the backward American design community. Certain china-painters, potters, and artists who came to see the exhibition were to play major roles in instigating an art pottery movement in the United States. Inspired by Oriental forms and glazes and by underglaze decorated ceramics from Haviland & Company of France and Doulton and Company of England, these visitors returned to their disparate homes and set about recreating similar wares on their own. In only a few years a ferment in ceramic-making was taking place. Interest in this type of work gained momentum and over the years evolved into a broadly based art pottery movement that continued in force until the dissipating upheavals of World War I.

In contrast to the folk and utilitarian potters who were struggling to preserve a long-standing tradition, American art potters had begun a new movement just before the time of Ohr's journey. Cincinnati was the most concentrated center, with Mary Louise McLaughlin, Thomas J. Wheatley, Rettig-Valentine, and the Rookwood Pottery. On the East Coast a more scattered development was taking place with Charles Volkmar, John Bennett, Odell & Booth Brothers, all in the New York City area, and the Chelsea Keramic Art Works in Chelsea, Massachusetts.

The majority of the new movement's members began as vessel decorators; virtually none of them made their own ware, or even knew how to use the potter's wheel. Individually hand-decorated pieces in underglaze slip technique (signed by the artist) seemed to satisfy the requirements for an anti-industrial aesthetic. It did not seem to matter that the forms they decorated were in some instances standardized shapes thrown by production potters and in others simply molded. For the most part, those who knew how to use the potter's wheel were considered skilled workmen rather than artists. Rookwood Pottery became the most famous of the early art pottery firms, and its operation exemplified this kind of division of labor between the artist who decorated the vessel and the workman who made it.

The early members of the art pottery movement, with the exception of Chelsea Keramic, totally focused their efforts on the technique of underglaze slip decoration. This technique consisted of painting a thick slip composed of clay, pigment, and water on the vessel in impasto and then firing it in the kiln. A second firing with an overall clear glaze produced a depth and brilliance reminiscent of oil painting. Floral motifs, the most popular subject matter, were painted on an eclectic variety of earthenware forms. Ohr's interest, however, was always with the potter's wheel rather than surface decoration. The craze for this style of decoration soon peaked, and the market became flooded with both domestic and imported wares. By 1884 numerous decorating workshops had reformed or closed their doors and Rookwood Pottery was in the process of substantially modifying its technique. In 1886 this resulted in the introduction of its Standard ware, a line decorated with backgrounds sprayed with soft gradations of colors. This elegant look promptly won gold medals, thus establishing Rookwood as the premier art pottery maker and setting off a rash of imitators.

The eclectic mix of Rookwood's early shapes—Japanese-inspired forms lifted from Emile

Figures 57–58
Below, Chinese T'ang dynasty bowl, 618–906, compared with an Ohr pot, below left, c. 1895–1900. T'ang vase: Museum of Fine Arts, Boston; Hoyt Collection. Ohr: Private collection, New York City.

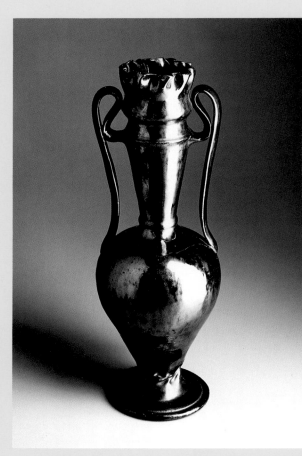

Gallé's faience as well as pillow vases and pil-
grim flasks, the flat sides of which functioned
as canvases for the decorators—gave way in the
late 1880s to vases and ewers with soft flowing
curves. In events apparently unrelated to Ohr,
an occasional Rookwood decorator tried his or
her hand at indenting or twisting the lip of the
still-damp vessel (Figure 68) he or she had been
given to work on.

The one exception to the widespread use of
underglaze decoration, and to a certain extent
the division of labor, was Chelsea Keramic,
which had been founded as early as 1872. By
the time of the Philadelphia Centennial in 1876
Chelsea Keramic had experimented with various aesthetic approaches to ceramics. Like
other ceramists they were spurred on to further
efforts by what they saw at the exhibition.

At Chelsea Keramic all the skills of the potter
were utilized. Followed by Ohr, the members of
the Robertson family, who founded the firm,
were among the first Americans to assume the
role of artist-potter, a role that gave them
complete aesthetic control over their work.
Chelsea Keramic's earliest approach to art pottery utilized fine red clay left in the bisque state.
Other techniques included molding, modeling,
carving, and incising; underglaze slip decorating, a minor interest inspired by the Centennial, was discontinued early on. Most relevant
to Ohr's future work would have been some of
their graceful Chinese-inspired, wheel-thrown
vessels—simple, elegant shapes, subtly glazed.
Occasionally these forms were gently manipulated by pinching or pulling (Figure 69), and
handles were sometimes used distinctively. By
1884, Chelsea Keramic's Hugh C. Robertson
had begun to focus his efforts solely on simple
Oriental-style forms and the re-creation of col-
orful, high-fired Oriental glazes, thus providing
the art pottery movement with an important
aesthetic alternative to underglaze slip decoration. Unfortunately his obsession with producing the elusive *sang-de-boeuf* glazes caused him
to bankrupt his company in 1889.

Having come to ceramics via the potter's wheel
rather than through painted decoration, Ohr
was in a rare position to explore the form of the
vessel, a fascination that in the early 1890s
prompted him to abandon Victorian ideas and
invent his own suprisingly modern concept of
form and decoration. Pieces from this period,
which perhaps began with the building of a
new kiln in 1888, were marked by impressing
various die-stamps (Figures 70, 71). Little of
this work exists because a fire wiped out Ohr's
studio in October 1894, but he was back in
business by January of 1895. The majority of
the work he is known for was produced after
that point until around 1900, and was impressed
with different die-stamps (Figure 72). At that
point, Ohr later recalled: "A visitor asked me
for my autograph and since then, 1898, my
creations are marked like a check"[18] (Figure 73).
He was, however, inconsistent in the first few
years, but then continued to incise the bottoms
of his pots until he retired around 1910.

For the Cotton Centennial Exhibition of 1884,
where he first launched his career publicly, Ohr
stated, "I had over 600 pieces, no two alike"[19]—
a telling remark that demonstrates the scale on
which he was thinking and suggests his driving
fascination with the unique. The fact that he

did not follow the traditional procedure of making standardized forms was highly unusual. Indeed in the context of the Industrial Revolution, when industry was mass producing more and more identical objects, the idea of "no two alike" was extraordinary. While individual pieces were created by members of the art pottery movement, more commonly they worked in series. No one adopted as extreme a standard as Ohr, who was proud that his work was incapable of being catalogued or duplicated.

The idea of making unique pieces was a significant concept that assumed larger proportions for Ohr as time went on, proving ultimately to be the motivation for his creativity and the vehicle of his greatness. We have no reason to conclude that Ohr, at this early stage, had yet conceived of making art pottery from an art-for-art's-sake point of view. "No two alike" no doubt meant making subtle variations on the wheel-thrown vessel or applying individual details, which simply reflected his craving for individuality. But he brought to ceramics a desire for personal expression far exceeding that of the typical art potter, and by repeatedly creating autonomous vessels, he continued to reassert and reaffirm his individuality. He was unequivocal on the subject: "I am the apostle of individuality, the brother of the human race, but I must be myself, and I want every vase of mine to be itself."[20]

At some point, Ohr was taken with the idea that the work of the craftsman could be construed as art. To achieve this goal, he felt the craftsman must act as an artist and the artist as a craftsman, doing all of his own work by hand. He explained, "Is This True—That all great 'actors' oritors 'musicians' 'sculptors' 'pugilists' 'poets'. . . must do their own work 2 score high meritorious recognition. If the above is true, then value the master potter's work as ceramic art proper."[21] Ohr's first experience at an art pottery may have come around 1886 when he was enlisted by the New Orleans Art Pottery, which had just been founded by William and Ellsworth Woodward, to help operate the pottery and make the ware.[22] By the time he constructed a new pottery in 1888,[23] if not before, he considered himself an art potter, and it was

Figures 62–63
Above, Greek red-figured vase (*Lekythos*), c. 450–500 B.C., attributed to the Quadrate Painter, compared with Ohr vase at left. Since the Greek piece was given to the Metropolitan Museum of Art in 1875 it may have been shown at their ceramics exhibition of the same year. Greek vase: The Metropolitan Museum of Art, New York; Gift of Samuel G. Ward, 1875. Ohr: See Plate 34.

in this year that he first issued his challenge "to meet any potter on earth in creating shapes,"[24] one that he maintained for the rest of his career.

There exist very few works from the 1880s, and even fewer dated ones, that shed light on Ohr's development during the critical period when he was firming up his identity as an art potter. The earliest dated piece after the pig flask is the 1886 pitcher with serpent spout (Figure 64). This pitcher, with its Italian Renaissance-style spout and the yellow and green mottled glaze that relates to European folk pottery, has a different character than his pieces from around 1890. Its heavy body and its emphasis on functional form embellished with artistic detail may represent a phase in which Ohr had not yet conceived of totally segregating the artistic from the useful. Another dated piece, a ewer form dated 1891 (Figure 75), is representative of a small group of vessels that also have heavily potted walls, but their decoration takes the form of finely tooled beading, small incised designs, and tooled concentric rings (Plate 2), or, occasionally, short molded handles with curlicues (Figure 76). For this group, a clear

Figure 64
Pitcher by Ohr, dated August 7, 1886. Robert Tannen, New Orleans.

Figure 65
Above, bowl by Christopher Dresser for Linthorpe Pottery of Middlesbrough, England, c. 1879–82. Private collection, New York City.

Figures 66–67
Below, Ohr vase, c. 1895–1900, with Linthorpe vase designed by Dresser, c. 1879–82, below right. Dresser: private collection, New York City. Ohr: Private collection, Montague, New Jersey.

glaze was used over a light-colored clay body to create a yellow ground; this occasionally was augmented with small amounts of color either splashed or applied decoratively with a sponge in the manner of American folk potters.

Since so few early pieces exist, it is necessary to analyze those that appear in an old photograph taken around 1890–92 of Ohr with an "ART POTTER" placard (Figure 2). The majority of the pieces pictured have complex ornamentation and are quite Victorian and neo-Rococo in their conception: rims are ruffled; flowers are applied in high relief; conventionalized leaf designs are embellished in low relief; pitcher spouts appear hand-formed; handles, both short and long, are molded with scrolls and curlicues. The vases in the upper and lower center of the photograph appear to have handles from the same mold as the vase in Figure 76. If the group of vessels that relate to the 1891 ewer and the group pictured in the old photo prove to be representative of Ohr's work from around 1888–92, we can see that, while

he was an entirely competent and inventive art potter, he had not yet broken away from contemporary concepts of pottery making. However, shortly after 1892 he largely discontinued the design characteristics identified with the 1880s, advanced the range of his glazes, and made a revolutionary breakthrough in form.

Ohr was right on cue with these changes, for the early 1890s was a time of transition in both mood and taste. The Victorian era following the Civil War has been termed the *Brown Decades* by Lewis Mumford,[25] who felt that the upheavals caused by the war, the assassination of Lincoln, and rapid industrialization had created a somber mood in the population. The result was subdued colors in decoration, buildings made of brownstone, and dark wood furnishings, all against a somber background of industrial grime.

By the mid-1890s, however, the Brown Decades had to give way to a brighter and more modern outlook, perhaps spurred on by the Chicago World's Columbian Exhibition, which took place in 1893. Although we have no evidence of how their work was received, two important members of the French art pottery movement, Ernest Chaplet and Auguste Delaherche, exhibited pieces at Chicago[26] largely based on Oriental forms but glazed with adventurous, high-fired colors developed from Chinese prototypes. Having persevered successfully, they had developed a wider range of glaze techniques than had Hugh C. Robertson up to the point of his bankruptcy. For his porcelain pieces, Chaplet created speckled, mottled, and crackled glazes, frequently in combinations of two or sometimes more colors such as red, turquoise, white, green, aubergine, and gray. Delaherche frequently favored large controlled drips of one color over another or combinations of a few colors flowing together such as red, olive, purple, green, or white for his stoneware.

After showing at the Chicago exhibition, Rookwood Pottery, which had contributed to the Brown Decades with its earth-toned Standard wares, responded to the changes in the air by adding three new brightly colored glazes in 1894. By the mid-1890s Hugh C. Robertson, now at Dedham Pottery, renewed his glaze experiments, continuing to develop his reds but augmenting them with green, blue, white, and other colors. He also created a finish that simulated lava flows by using multiple firings to produce thick accumulations of glazes. Newcomb Pottery, a new entrant to the art pottery movement, readily adopted blue, green, white, and cream in its painted decoration of stylized floral motifs.

The concept of integrating ornament or decoration with the structure of the vessel also seems to have stirred great interest. Some ceramic makers were no longer content with decorative painting that merely lay on the surface of the form or with applied decoration that jutted extraneously from it. Between 1891 and 1893, Kate B. Sears set a precedent for working in porcelain when she carved exquisite scenes on vases for the Ceramic Art Company, predecessor of the Lenox China Company of Trenton, New Jersey. Around the same time, Susan Frackelton of Milwaukee abandoned china decorating for the potter's wheel in order to make her own stoneware forms for modeling and carving. By the time of the Chicago exhibition, she had progressed sufficiently to win a gold medal. Other decorators followed her example as they realized that they needed control over the shape to successfully integrate carving and incising into wet clay. While this need brought more ceramists to the potter's wheel in the late 1890s, at the time of the Chicago exhibition in 1893 Ohr had been at the potter's wheel for well over a decade.

Reportedly Ohr exhibited his ceramics at Chicago.[27] Up until that time he had largely employed the simple concepts and glaze materials of contemporary folk potters, but around these years he expanded his low-fired color and glazing techniques to feature green, yellow, mauve, and dark blood-red. Frequently, Ohr also used a single color with spattered black speckles. How much influence the exhibits had on him remains to be seen, but surely the glazes there must have set a standard for the use of bright colors in combination. Ohr's approach to low-

Figure 68
Below far left, vase by the Rookwood Pottery Company of Cincinnati, decorated by Kate C. Machette in 1892. The indenting we see here was actually quite atypical of Rookwood's work. Robert W. Skinner Gallery, Bolton, Massachusetts.

Figure 69
Below, vase on the left by Ohr, c. 1895–1900, and one on the right by the Chelsea Keramic Art Works of Chelsea, Massachusetts. Private collection, New York City.

fired speckled glazes somewhat resembles the results of Chaplet's high-fired technique, although it may have connections to spattering techniques used earlier in the nineteenth century.

When Ohr developed his radically manipulated approach in the early 1890s, he not only gave vessels a sculptural presence, but developed a unique, idiosyncratic approach to integrating ornament with structure. Unlike others who carved, incised, or modeled stylized subjects from nature on their vessels, the Biloxi potter created abstract, structural elements that did not represent anything from the objective world. Yet after laying bare this conceptually exciting field and commencing work, Ohr was struck by tragedy. On October 12, 1894, a large fire swept much of downtown Biloxi and destroyed the kiln, workshop, and most of his work. Ohr salvaged a number of his "burned babies" from the rubble; an examination of some of these surviving pieces confirms that he had created a sizable body of manipulated work at some point after the Victorian work of 1888–92 and just prior to the fire (Figures 77–81). Also among the salvaged pieces were functional ware, souvenir ware, and vessels that indicate that he had begun to throw thinner walled pots.

Ohr's creative inspiration during these years must have been fed by the spirit of change that so strongly marked the 1890s, but we might also imagine that he felt pressure from his self-imposed concept of "no two alike" to continue creating unique forms. After throwing many thousands of vessels with only the subtle variations that the potter's wheel allows, Ohr might have looked fondly on any accident or deviation that occurred in his work—some deviation that would stimulate new possibilities and expand the range of his shapes. In his earliest art pottery he had already performed mild manipulations when he followed the tradition of the folk potters in ruffling the rims of vases and in hand-forming the spouts of pitchers. The opportunity to push this tendency further may have come when Ohr began to throw vessels with thinner walls. A frequent culmination of the attempt to throw more thinly is a weakening of the pot wall, for as the wall becomes thinner and more moist it loses strength. When the pot can no longer resist the centrifugal force it begins to twist and ultimately collapses. Ohr must have been fascinated by the possibilities of collapsed vessels and the unique way in which the collapsed wall integrates a decorative quality into the structure. With numerous small precedents in his mind, he may have felt confident in expanding these accidents into premeditated manipulation.

Figures 70–74
Ohr's marks, from top to bottom: early period, c. 1888–94 (used prior to the fire of October 1894); early period, c. 1888–94 (all pieces with this mark are pre-October 1894); middle period, c. 1895–1900 (this mark is the most common); late period, c. 1898–1910; all periods.

Ohr dug his fingers into the moist, plastic clay of his finely thrown pieces. In place of the traditional smooth and symmetrical contour of the vessel, he induced asymmetrical and three-dimensional configurations into the surface by altering the structure: twisting, folding, indenting, crinkling, ruffling, lobing, off-centering, and conjoining. He impregnated each form with some variation of his new, private vision, on occasion using two, three, or even four different types of manipulations on the same piece.

Ohr's work ranges from the simple to the radical, and encompasses variations including applied handles, reticulated carving, applied three-dimensional reptiles, and, rarely, incised decoration by Ohr or his foster son, John Harry Portman. Many of his manipulated vessels are traditional forms that have been modified only gently by a slight twisting of the rim or by a modest indentation of the midsection. One group of vases, however, is unprecedented in spite of having no manipulation. These wheel-thrown pieces have unusual convoluted profiles in baluster form that can be read as stacked pots. Ohr threw some of them as one continuous piece: one vase shape on the top of another vase shape (Plates 37, 38, 39, 43).

However, it is only in the extreme versions with deep and heavy manipulations that the revolutionary aspect of Ohr's approach is dramatically revealed (Plates 64, 76, 118). Ohr honored the wheel-thrown, hollow vessel as his starting point much in the way that a painter accepts his two-dimensional canvas. He re-formed the vessel with three-dimensional structural changes and shifted the focus of interest from simple outline or embellished decoration to design elements that were incorporated into the structure. The original symmetrical wheel-thrown form was altered by three-dimensionality in strategic ways, and a new spatial dialogue was created between the remnants of the original contour and the more complex abstract spaces. Ohr explored form in a profound way that transcended the vessel, one that demanded a re-

Figures 75–76
Far left, ewer form by Ohr, inscribed June 20, 1891. Left, vase with molded handles by Ohr, c. 1890–92. Far left: Private collection, New York City. Left: Andrew Van Styn, Chicago.

79

sponse far more complex than that accorded to most art pottery. Although there was no historical precedent at that time for viewing vessels as sculpture, his work has a definite sculptural aspect.

How did Ohr create and sustain such an inventive, gestural language and produce such a variety of forms? Thinking of him as a traditional craftsman does not begin to explain the level of genius he reached as one of the great fin de siècle artists. In reference to mid-twentieth century art, Anton Ehrenzweig has written, "The modern artist attacks his own rational sensibilities in order to make room for spontaneous growth."[28] But rational thinking, like gravity, eventually reasserts itself, and a cycle of struggle ensues.

It is the intuitive, spontaneous moment, Ehrenzweig suggests, that gives a work of art a vital and suprising nature. Ohr spoke of the intuitive nature of his own creativity when he said, "Shapes come to the potter as verses come to the poet."[29] Yet his artistic creativity also expressed a certain fatherly impulse; indeed he often referred to his vessels as his "clay babies." According to Ohr, "Each piece of pottery I make is a baby. I brood over it with the same tenderness a mortal child awakens in its parents."[30] This vision of mortal individuality that Ohr attached to his pots is reflected in his interpretation of the Bible. "According to the Good Book, we are created from clay," he wrote, "and as Nature had it so destined that no two of us are alike, all couldn't be symmetrically formed, caused a variety to be wabble-jawed, hare-lipped, cross-eyed, all colors, bow-legged, knock-kneed, extra limbs, also minus of the

Figures 77–81
Right and opposite page, vessels retrieved from the rubble after Ohr's studio burned, c. 1893–94. Although it is not known exactly when Ohr first began to manipulate vessels into unusual shapes, these pieces demonstrate that he had begun by at least the early 1890s. Private collection, New York City.

same, all sizes from 30 inches to 75 ditto. Every one of us sees different, has a different voice, and don't all like cabbage or chew tobacco! . . . I make disfigured pottery—couldn't and wouldn't if I could make it any other way."[31]

Ohr's force as an artist emerged from a rare combination of factors. His intense creative drive and his passionate individualism expressed themselves in his uncompromising conviction that true art can come only from "the hand of the maker," a conviction that marked him as an artist to a degree seldom encountered in the art pottery movement. Ohr's rejection of industrial methods reflected the ideas of John Ruskin, who railed against the evils of machine production and praised the animated beauty of handcrafted art. But Ruskin's philosophy did not infiltrate the American design community until late in the 1890s, through the English Arts and Crafts Movement and the writings of William Morris—years behind Ohr. While Morris's serious concerns for social reform were not imported to the States, the promise of finding joy through handiwork in the creation of household objects plus the challenge of combining utility and beauty, humble materials and honest construction, drew Americans to the Arts and Crafts Movement and the decorative arts. These seductive features inspired the creation of Arts and Crafts societies in cities across the country, beginning in 1897 with the foundation of the Boston Society of Arts and Crafts. Infused with these new ideas, the art pottery movement mushroomed in the years around the turn of the century.

Idealism ran high in the Arts and Crafts Movement, and a new wave of decorators and newcomers took command of the potter's wheel, among them Charles F. Binns, Mary Louise McLaughlin, William J. Walley, and Adelaide Alsop Robineau. The realities of making handmade objects in a competitive, highly industrialized society, however, produced inevitable compromises. Paradoxically, at the peak of the Arts and Crafts influence around 1900, just when these new artist-potters had eliminated the division of labor in their work, competitive forces began to cause other makers (Van Briggle Pottery, the Gates Potteries, Tiffany Studios) to employ industrial techniques for creating art

pottery. By making a mold from one prototype many replicas could be cast very economically, thus eliminating even hand decoration. While the results of these efforts were apparently accepted as art pottery at the time, in the context of Arts and Crafts philosophy the irony is now overwhelming.

Since it was far easier for ceramic makers to adhere to design principles than work ethics, the design simplicity fostered by the Arts and Crafts Movement gained momentum in the late 1890s. Austerity became the new authority in place of the complex Victorian clutter of the 1880s. Flat patterns stylized from nature were exemplified by Newcomb Pottery and later, by Marblehead Pottery of Marblehead, Massachusetts. The work of Binns, Walley, and Robineau in her early period updated the Oriental concept of simple forms with harmonious glazes to fit in with the tendencies of the Arts and Crafts Movement. Spelling out the new stylistic goals, the Boston Arts and Crafts Society charter specified, "This Society was incorporated . . . to counteract . . . the desire for over-ornamentation and specious originality. It will insist upon . . . sobriety and restraint."[32] While this new spirit was directed at Victorian design and not at Ohr, it was indicative of changes that no doubt contributed to the further stylistic isolation of his work, for although he made simple forms that were simply glazed, this was a minority of his efforts.

An alternative to painted or glazed decoration was offered by the Grueby Pottery Company in 1897. Grueby's new technique largely consisted of simple leaf patterns modeled in low relief on the surface and repeated around the vessel, an ensemble of form and pattern that was unified by a newly developed mat glaze. This glaze was thick, devoid of gloss, and slightly textured. Grueby created a sensation by mainly relying on greens, ranging from forest to apple, and the work was an instant success, spawning a number of imitators as had Rookwood's Standard ware a decade earlier. Ironically, although Grueby's work was praised as the epitome of the Arts and Crafts influence, it was created with a greater division of labor than was used by Rookwood; there, designers were at least allowed to conceive of their own designs, while

at Grueby, designers were required to execute patterns created by a head designer.

With Grueby's success the mat glaze became firmly associated with Arts and Crafts design, and around 1900 it began to be widely used. Ohr was not immune to this vogue, although the mat glaze remained a very minor aspect of his work. An analysis of his pieces with autograph mark shows that he developed his own mat and semi-mat glazes during the last decade he worked. Unlike Grueby's practice of covering nearly everything with green, Ohr maintained his taste for red and for bright combinations of colors.

Despite Grueby's new approach, the popularity of painted decoration derived from nature as well as Oriental form and glaze hung on tenaciously. Arts and Crafts idealism and commercialism continued to gain momentum side by side. The exaggerated floral style of ornamentation frequently associated with Continental art nouveau was touched on only gingerly: Van Briggle molded a substantial number of vases in the art nouveau style; Rookwood and Newcomb Pottery experimented with it in a minor portion of their painted decoration; and McLaughlin made restrained interpretations with her carved *Losanti* porcelains. Except for Ohr's experimental work, form in America for the most part remained tied to the simpler Oriental prototypes and to basic wheel-thrown shapes.

The unfolding of Ohr's career positioned him as a witness to an evolution in styles as well as the ebb and flow of idealism about the production of art pottery. The Arts and Crafts Movement brought a needed infusion of idealism to the art pottery movement. But after years of exemplifying the ideal of the principled craftsman in the true spirit of the Arts and Crafts vision with his commitment to making handmade art pottery, Ohr's complex conception of form came into conflict with the movement's new stylistic goals of sparse simplicity.

The idealism of the art pottery movement in general, which had previously failed to meet Ohr's strict standards, fell further behind with the introduction of industrial methods. Ohr

was critical. He condemned the lack of originality, the division of labor, the use of industrial techniques for molding art pottery, and the lack of "the hand of the maker" traceable to one artist (such as himself) rather than to a dozen factory hands. As he put it:

no real "ART Pottery is now CREATED . . . . the MACHINE ART Works—is a fake and Fraud. . . . G. E. OHR Will and can Make any of the high Priced Payers—of Rookwood Teco—Vanbriggle . . ." "show their HAND—As to where is the Potter—that can" "FATHER the Art Produced—The out-come would "BE" that Five-or Fifteen Did the" Job on Pot . . . . it Dont Take A Doz to Accomplish Art Pottery— (Originality does not Emanate from a Company or a regiment(.[33]

By the time the fire of 1894 had forced him to start over, Ohr had three significant developments in place: a concept of manipulated form, a broader range of glazes, and a growing ability to throw eggshell-thin vessels. Apparently he bounced back from the tragedy of the fire with renewed energy, for in 1895 he was photographed with a large placard that read "'GREATEST' ART POTTER ON EARTH— 'YOU' PROVE THE CONTRARY" (Figure 14). His grandiose confidence was still in ascendancy, and he flourished. As this extraordinary potter continued his work in the late 1890s, innovations flowed freely; functional requirements were ignored. He routinely threw ultra-lightweight vessels fragile as eggshells and perilously complex with protrusions and serpentine handles. He induced fluidity and elongation into his handles—handles that were like drawings in the air—and developed a virtuosity for applying those long, sinuous extrusions.

Ohr continued to use the local, low-fired earthenware that he himself dug in the bayous or occasionally picked up in city streets. And, as we have mentioned, he continued to broaden his palette and expand his approach to glazing. Sponged and spattered applications frequently appeared with brighter colors. On occasion he anticipated *fauve*-like color with brilliant combinations, on others he continued using sober monochromes. He also developed subtle, soft, iridescent, metallic glazes as well as heavily textured lava glazes. Ohr's idiosyncrasy went as far as applying a different glaze to each side of certain vessels, usually with one side bland or dull and the other active or bright. Some pots were even covered with three or four different glazes, side by side.

An unusual development after 1900 was Ohr's creation of a large body of work left in the bisque or unglazed state. Dated pieces suggest that the majority of these vessels were made between the years 1902 and 1907, although it was reported as early as 1899 that "he shows quaintly distorted unglazed pieces."[34] Ceramics made from finely textured red clay and left in the bisque state had been a significant aspect of American art pottery of the mid–1870s. Its initial appeal was soon eclipsed by the new taste for underglaze slip decoration and for monochromatic, Oriental-style glazes. At the time of Ohr's bisque production, the only significant maker of this type of ware was Roblin Art Pottery in California, founded in 1898 by Alexander W. Robertson, formerly of Chelsea Keramic.

Perhaps Ohr's emphasis on bisque ware was a reaction to critics who praised his glazes and had nothing good to say about his shapes. Since he had felt all along that his real genius lay in the area of form, he shrugged off the praise and refused to take credit for the glazes, calling them accidents and blaming the results on the mysteries of firing the kiln. Yet although Ohr may have made a conscious aesthetic decision to leave a large portion of his new work unglazed, he may have left others unglazed because he had lost heart during these twilight years as a potter for continuing an unrewarded career.

Among Ohr's bisque ware was a group of small, quickly made vessels and trinkets that most likely were left unglazed to be sold cheaply as souvenirs. There are also imperfect, misfired, and damaged pieces that Ohr compulsively saved. As he explained, "Did you ever hear of a mother so inhuman that she would cast off her deformed child?"[35] Additionally, a large group of bisque ware exists, ranging from simple bowls to the most complex manipulated shapes. A small portion of the latter group stands out, the most striking examples of which were made from scroddled or marbleized clay (two or more colors of clay blended together). Perhaps these pieces were meant to focus attention solely upon his new feeling for form, freed from the distraction of the glaze. Most frequently these pieces are bowl forms that have been manipulated with new types of curving undulations and swirls (Plates 79, 80, 82, 83). These asymmetrical, self-contained designs lead the eye to and fro among rhythmic, reciprocal elements, a feature that is quite distinct from Ohr's earlier crinkled pieces with their random intent, and from his folded pieces with their angular and sometimes symmetrical presence. They reflect Ohr's further refinement of his concept of the sculptural vessel. This last advance carried Ohr even further from the mainstream. These freeform shapes, which now lacked the common denominator of glaze, had moved further toward deserting the traditional vessel. The sole remaining element in common with works from the art pottery movement was the circular base, denoting that the piece had originated on the potter's wheel.

Although Ohr responded to the general aesthetic and conceptual changes that affected the ceramics community, his response was always idiosyncratic, leaving him an outsider in America throughout his career, an unrecognized genius whose vision isolated him from the puzzled world around him. If we place Ohr's work in the larger context of European decorative arts, however, it may seem less aberrant than it did in America. While he was never directly exposed to Continental art nouveau, for instance, many elements of his work have a greater kinship to that aesthetic than to anything in the United States. Perhaps if he had lived in Paris rather than in Biloxi, he might have been accepted as one of the greatest artists of La Belle Epoque.

By the 1890s the Continent was the home of a variety of artistic movements and the center of many conceptual and aesthetic experiments, which generally reached America in a frail, diluted condition. Although Ohr may have been vaguely aware of Continental work, his own experiments with form developed independently of European currents. Nevertheless, it is well to note that chronologically the development of his most radical work in the early

1890s paralleled the rise of the most advanced concepts there, and the rich unfolding of his mature work in the second half of the 1890s paralleled a peak period in Continental decorative arts. Ohr, it seems, partook of the spirit of the age. In this larger context, it might be appropriate to view his work as a probing search for new parameters for the field of ceramics under the permissive license given the decorative arts in the quest for aesthetic renewal.

On the Continent, artists may have been encouraged to experiment with the decorative arts by the theoretical ideas put forth in England that proposed that design be viewed on a par with the fine arts.[36] They carried on the English search for a new style, for ways to express constructive principles, and for new ways to interpret nature. During the 1870s a fascination with Japanism had provided exotic stimulation and injected new elements into the design arena. With English design philosophy based on neo-Gothic principles permeating the Continent, the raging influence of Japanism, along with the influences of the Symbolist movement and the Rococo Revival, interacted with the vogue for naturalism. Nature was stylized through Japanism and given subjective meaning through Symbolism. A sinuous use of line was developed and asymmetry was adopted from both Japanism and the neo-Rococo. In the early 1890s this complex interaction of influences produced the short-lived art nouveau style. Although the line between Japanism and art nouveau is occasionally still as fuzzy as it was during the 1890s, it is safe to say that Japanism survived independently during this era and into the twentieth century.

Even though English design theories were seminal for the development of Continental art nouveau, England did not participate in the movement except in a minor way. There are, however, a few English ceramic forms that share the Japanism that so influenced the French potters during the era of the 1890s and, interestingly enough, certain of these relate to the way in which the Biloxi potter worked. While examples from Martin Brothers and Doulton and Company in England are enticingly similar to his work, it is not known to what degree they were exploring the earlier precedents of the

Figure 82
Above, vase by Ohr, c. 1895–1900, compared with vase attributed to Edward Martin of Martin Brothers, London and Southall, England, 1894. Private collection, New York City.

Figure 83
Martin Brothers vase, dated 7–1900. Private collection, New York City.

Japanese or of their fellow Englishman, Christopher Dresser. Either might also have been aware of Ohr's work, but more likely this was merely coincidence.

Edwin Martin of the Martin Brothers workshop in Southall began to interpret gourd forms with his vessels at least by 1894, and went on to create further "abstractions from nature,"[37] with pots that simulated textures like barks, skins, scales, and corrugated surfaces. The organic ensemble presented by these vessels compares favorably with an organic type of Japanism pursued by many of the French potters of the same period. On other works Martin appears to have briefly abandoned nature's representational guideposts to experiment with nonrepresentational techniques such as twisting and squashing. "Marred in the hand of the potter - Jer - 18 - 4," Martin inscribed one misshapen pot, thus invoking a different Biblical justification than the one Ohr offered for his work. A few Martin pieces with elaborate structural manipulation come close to rivaling the curious power of Ohr's forms (Figures 82, 83).

Another example of English work that bears a strong similarity to some of Ohr's pieces can be seen in the production of Doulton and Company of Lambeth. Around 1897 Mark V. Marshall and perhaps other Doulton artists modeled a few vases using deep twists and other manipulations similar to Ohr's own approach (Figure 84). While the piece illustrated is nicely sculptural in feeling, its power is diluted by Doulton's proclivity for adding ornament in the form of neo-Rococo floral cartouches, executed with a squeeze-bag technique and covered with a glossy glaze.

Of all the Western potters of the epoch, it is the work of the French ceramists, largely based on Japanese-inspired gourd shapes, that offers the most pertinent comparison with Ohr's work. The French learned to internalize the design principles inherent in Japanese work and began to perceive relationships between Japanese vessels and nature.[38] A number of these potters began to interpret nature themselves, creating vessels reminiscent of gourds, vegetables, and fruit. The manner in which the subtle, abstract

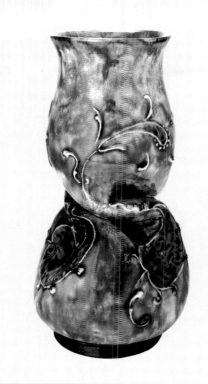

qualities of contour, color, texture, and frequently asymmetry coalesced in a vessel emerged as a new emphasis. In America few potters took this route, although examples of the style can be found in the work of Chelsea Keramic, Grueby Pottery, and Tiffany Studios, and it was introduced by the French potter, Taxile Doat, into the work of University City Pottery, which was founded late in the era.

Stylistic matters are seldom neat and tidy. Many French ceramic makers moved back and forth between the influences of Japanism, naturalism, Symbolism, art nouveau, and the vast heritage of Chinese forms and glazes. Thus a rich and diverse body of work was created during the years between 1895 and 1905, roughly the same period as Ohr's mature phase. Although Ohr's pieces with extreme manipulations defy comparison, a portion of his work does offer a bit of common ground with French work through details of construction: bulges, lobes, cavities, dents, creases, twists, and undulating curves. Yet the close parallels in these comparisons belie the wide gulf that separates his inventive structural manipulations from the limited possibilities of interpreting natural forms.

Figures 84–85
Above left, vase by Doulton & Company of Lambeth, England, c. 1897, executed by Mark V. Marshall, compared with Ohr vase at right, c. 1895–1900. Private collections, New York.

Ohr's unexpected approach to the plastic possibilities of clay produced work possessing magically organic qualities. His organic symbols, cut adrift from nature, exude a perplexing symbolism that has nothing in common with motifs abstracted from nature or with the Symbolist movement in which carefully conceived imagery was purposely designed to evoke illusive yet allusive meaning. Ohr's shapes were unreminiscent. His experiments with construction produced surprising structural details that provoked unpredictable ornamentation, as if the "bare, stark personality in every jar and jug"[39] were trying to communicate the artist's deepest, inexpressible, inarticulate secrets through the magic syntax of form.

Figure 86
Vases by Ohr, c. 1895–1900, left, and by Jean Carriès, c. 1889–94, right. Private collection, New York City.

Figure 87
Vase by the French potter Auguste Delaherche, c. 1887–94, below left, compared with similar piece by Ohr, c. 1895–1900. Private collection, New York City.

The sheer variety in French work during this period makes possible some interesting comparisons. In addition to the work of Jean Carriès (Figure 86), Auguste Delaherche (Figure 87), Abbé Pacton (Figure 88), and Sèvres (Figure 89), it is fascinating to note that comparisons also can be made with the work of Ernest Chaplet, Taxile Doat, Henry-Léon-Charles Robalbhen, Alexandre Bigot, Emile Grittel, Georges Hoentschel, Paul Jeanneney, Pierre Adrien Dalpayrat, and Emil Decouer.

If we consider the work of certain designers and architects of that period, such as Victor Horta and Henry Van de Velde of Belgium, Hector Guimard of France, and Antonio Gaudí of Spain, we find work that exhibits a free-play attitude toward form and structure and that powerfully evokes Ohr's own aesthetic. In each man's work, nature at some point was abstracted, transcended, or rejected. Horta indicated his position when he wrote: "I leave the flower and the leaf, and I take the stalk."[40] His aim was to educe power and character from the sap-laden energy of the universal stem, leaving behind the identifiable contours of flowers and leaves. In a similar vein Guimard created a language of fantastic horticultural forms. For his design for the Paris Metro he processed plant forms into molten organic heraldry and tenuous skeins embracing asymmetrical, over-sized ovum.

Although Gaudí and Ohr had no contact and never worked in the same media, both were possessed by equally eccentric spirits and by equally radical urges that led them to produce unprecedented forms. Although Gaudí extrapolated the majority of his forms from Gothic, Moorish, and natural prototypes, it appears that at certain moments he was able to transcend these ties and produce nonrepresentational shapes. The unpredictable aspect of Gaudí's work is grandly demonstrated by the roof terrace of the Casa Mila (Figure 90), a veritable menagerie of abstract forms, which are, in fact, chimneys. As we can see, Gaudí and Ohr shared the feeling for unpredictable forms produced by the magic of turning structural details into ornament.

Ohr had a conceptual approach in common with the designer Henry Van de Velde, although their work itself was totally different. They both sidestepped the dead-end approach of deriving ornament from natural forms, and created ornament through structure. According to Van de Velde, "The least sentimental weakness, the least naturalistic association, weakens the lasting nature of. . .ornament."[41] Van de Velde's art nouveau designs have a cool, complex interplay of abstract form and line, but in these elements he has completely eliminated all references to nature. Claiming that the function of ornament was not to decorate but to structure, he declared, "The relations between this 'structural and dynamographic' ornament and the form or the surfaces, should appear so intimate that the ornament seems to have 'determined' the form"[42]—a theory that seems to describe accurately Ohr's approach.

If a tangible link existed between Ohr's concepts and those produced by the ferment in the Continental decorative arts, there would be a ready and reasonable explanation for his remarkable aesthetic development way down in Biloxi. Ohr's nearest link was his circumstantial connection with Christopher Dresser. It is tempting to try to link Dresser to the Continent, since he anticipated by at least a decade the Japanism of the French ceramists in the 1890s. He also anticipated by about two decades the art nouveau concept of abstracting dynamic elements from nature such as Horta discussed with "the stalk." As early as 1873, Dresser wrote about exploiting the symbolic sources of power: "I have employed such lines as we see in the bursting buds of spring, when the energy of growth is at its maximum."[42] Although similar ideas were in the air and underpinned the work on the Continent, there is, however, no evidence that Dresser was the direct source.

After all the comparisons, then, all the analyses of parallels, and the search for European connections, it appears that we must give back to George Ohr his uniqueness. He remains a homegrown, American anomaly.

To assess Ohr's status in the larger European context, developments in nineteenth-century decorative arts must be juxtaposed with those in the exalted fine arts of the modern era. During the 1890s, the more sophisticated designers, painters, and sculptors of the day began to employ personal artistic styles that had been created by subjectively abstracting from nature. No matter how abstract their work became, however, nature remained to define the limits. Yet the conceptual approach developed in this volatile decade by Ohr and certain Continental designers (Guimard, Gaudí, Van de Velde), transcended this limitation. Perhaps they were driven by fantasy; perhaps they pursued abstraction so far that they fell through a magic mirror into a realm that reflected nothing of nature, a realm of pure nonrepresentational form. This development in the decorative arts anticipated a similar twentieth-century approach that led to nonobjective work in the fine arts, first by Wassily Kandinsky and then by the Constructivist movement. Perhaps not until the Constructivists were nonrepresentational, three-dimensional objects first made in the fine arts; cubism, no matter how abstract, remained conceptually tied to the world of objects and figures.

In his highly subjective, gestural approach, Ohr also anticipated an intuitive mode of creativity that in the twentieth century became known as Expressionism. And in the field of ceramics his work was so avant garde that the concept of manipulating vessels was not rediscovered until some forty-five years after his retirement. Although he intuitively created art that was far in advance of its time, raising his ceramic work to the level of true art and even exceeding that of the most progressive Europeans, Ohr failed to receive recognition for his achievement. The obstacles standing in the way were created not only by the work but by Ohr himself. Because he was convinced that he had made an important contribution, he concluded that his cache of six thousand pieces was inseparable. "My object is [to] dispose of the whole collection to one creature or one country!" he wrote in 1901. ". . .My creations shall not! will not! and wont be sold separate."[43] Since he had boasted that he was unable to duplicate himself, a piece sold would be a piece lost; Ohr no doubt felt

Figures 88–89
Vase by Abbé Pierre Pacton, France, c. 1900, above, and, below, by the Sèvres Manufactory, France, dated 1900. Private collection, New York City.

that the impact of his achievement would be diluted if the collection were dispersed piecemeal. On some occasions Ohr was willing to make concessions by selling individual pieces, however it was reported, "He has a unique way of valuing goods. He wants their weight in gold . . . not because he is grasping enough to care for so much money, but as a test of your appreciation of true art."[44] The sensationalism of these demands worked against Ohr. In addition, his exhibitionism, his visual and verbal punning, and the heavy-handed hyperbole he employed in signs, handbills, and pronouncements also raised doubts in his contemporaries' minds about the seriousness of his work.

But the grandiose tests and goals that Ohr concocted for his work merely clouded the issue. His work was serious, and he encountered major difficulties because his forms were alien and perplexing. The art historian George Kubler has described the difficulty that truly innovative work encounters. "For most persons inventive behavior is a lapse of propriety surrounded by the frightening aura of a violation of the sanctity of routine. . . ." he explains. "Many societies have accordingly proscribed all recognition of inventive behavior, preferring to reward ritual repetition, rather than to permit inventive variations. . . .The human situation admits invention only as a very difficult tour de force. . . ."[45]

Ohr was well aware that he had made an important contribution to ceramic history, and indeed to art history in general. Although he probably had no inkling of the subtle contextual connections we have suggested, he only needed to look about to see that there was no body of work that could match his for radical originality. His proclamations touting these achievements were ridiculed by the public; critics loved his glazes while disparaging his revolutionary manipulation of form. But George Ohr was right: he *was*, as he claimed, the "Unequalled! Unrivalled! Undisputed! Greatest Art Potter on Earth!"[46]

Figure 90
Antonio Gaudí's Casa Mila in Barcelona, 1906–10—a veritable menagerie of abstract forms, which are, in fact, chimneys. Giant bell shapes with radiating lobes and others with concave facets stand near lopsided whorls that terminate in bizarre protrusions and large rectangular blocks that twist up to sprout chimney spires.

Plate 36   Vase, c. 1898–1907. Height: 8¾ inches. Private collection, New York City.

Plate 37   Vase, c. 1895–1900. Height: 11¼ inches. Private collection, New York.

Plate 38   Tall vase, c. 1895–1900. Height: 13½ inches. Private collection, New York City.

Plate 39
Tall vase, c. 1898–1907.
Height: 13½ inches. Private collection,
New York City.

Plate 40
Vase, c. 1895–1900.
Height: 7⅝ inches. Private collection,
New York.

Plate 41
Bowl, c. 1895–1900.
Height: 4⅞ inches. Private collection, New York City.

Plate 42
Footed vase, c. 1895–1900.
Height: 6⅜ inches. Private collection, New York.

Plate 43   Tall vase, c. 1895–1900. Height: 13 inches. Tom Dillenberg and Judy Espinar, New York City.

Plate 44
Handled vase, c. 1898–1907.
Height: 7 ⅜ inches. Private collection, New York City.

Plate 45
Handled vase, c. 1895–1900.
Height: 8 inches. Private collection, New York.

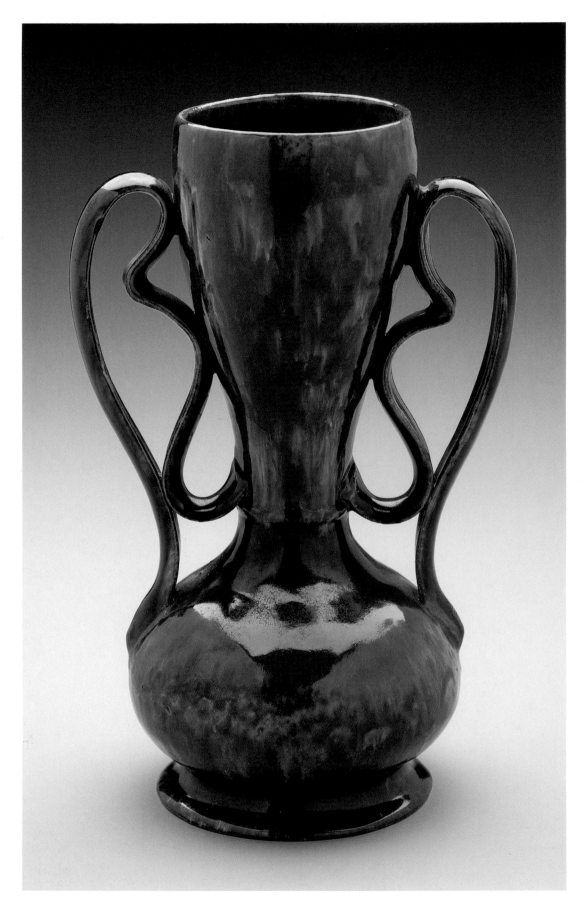

Plate 46   Handled vase, c. 1895–1900. Height: 7¾ inches. Private collection, New York.

Plate 47   Handled vase, c. 1895–1900. Height: 9½ inches. Private collection, New York City.

Plate 48   Tall handled vase, c. 1900. Height: 11⅜ inches. Private collection, New York City.

Plate 49
Pitcher, c. 1898–1907.
Height: 4¾ inches. Private collection, New York.

Plate 50
Pitcher, c. 1895–1900.
Height: 5½ inches. Private collection, New York.

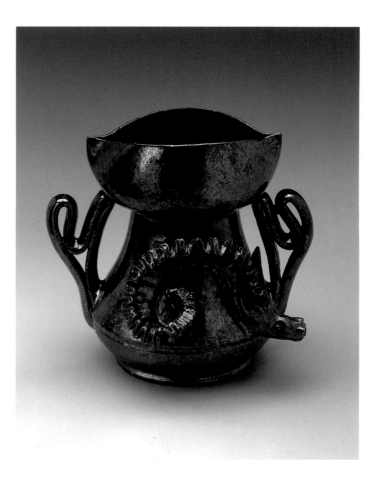

Plate 51
Handled vase with snake, c. 1895–1900.
Height: 4⅛ inches. Private collection, New York City.

Plate 52
Small pitcher, c. 1898.
Height: 3 inches. Charles Cowles, New York City.

Plate 53
Small pitcher, c. 1895–1900.
Height: 3¾ inches. Private collection, New York.

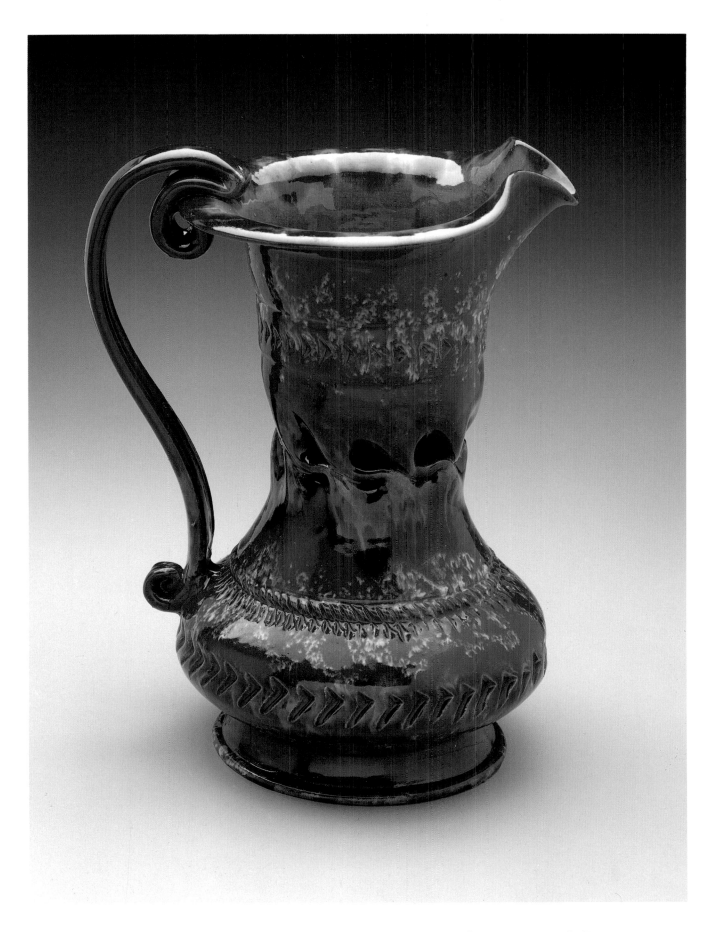

Plate 54   Pitcher, c. 1895–1900.   Height: 8 inches. Private collection, New York City.

Plate 55   Pitcher, c. 1895–1900. Height: 8⅝ inches. Private collection, New York City.

Plate 56
Pitcher, c. 1898–1907.
Height: 4¼ inches. Private collection, New York City.

Plate 57
Pitcher, c. 1895–1900.
Height: 6½ inches. Private collection, New York.

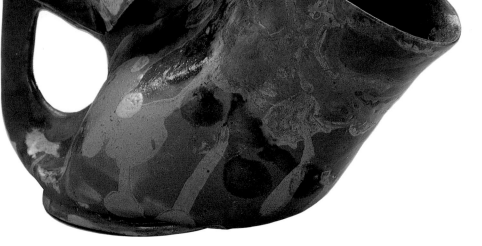

Plate 58
Pitcher, c. 1895–1900.
Height: 3 inches. Private collection, New York City.

Plate 59
Pitcher, c. 1898–1907.
Height: 3⅝ inches. Private collection, New York City.

Plate 60
Pitcher, c. 1898–1907.
Height: 3½ inches. Betty and Robert Hut,
New York City.

Plate 61   Pitcher, c. 1895–1900. Height: 5 inches. Private collection, New York.

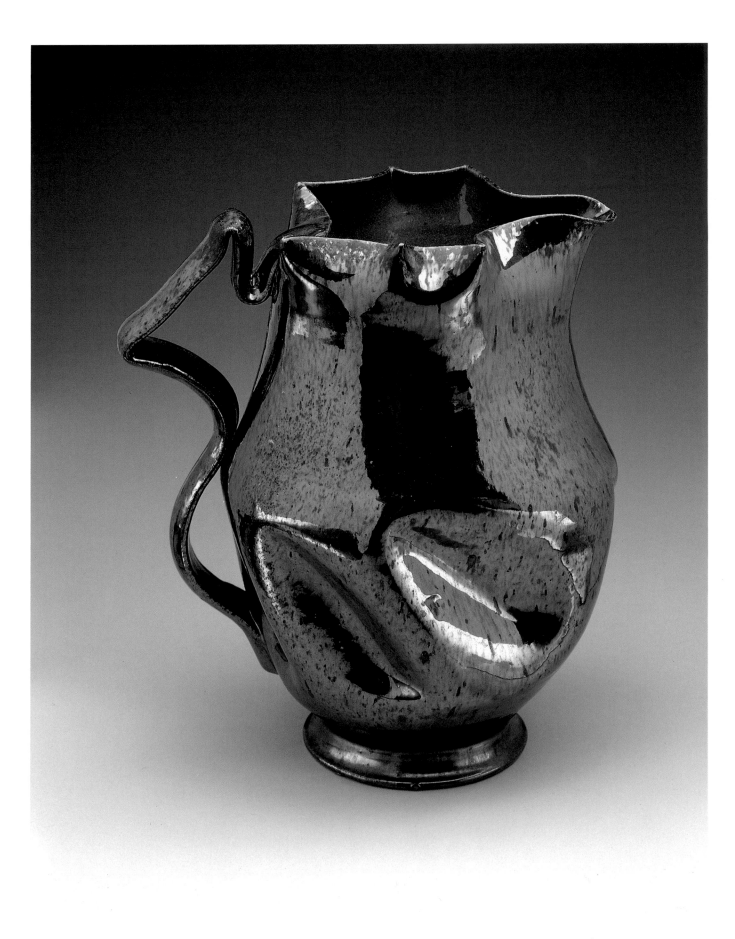

Plate 62   Pitcher, c. 1895–1900. Height: 9¼ inches. Private collection, New York City.

Plate 63   Pitcher with snake, c. 1895–1900. Height: 7 inches. Private collection, New York.

Plate 64
Vase, c. 1900.
Height: 8 inches, Jederman N.A., Princeton,
New Jersey.

Plate 65
Vase, c. 1895–1900.
Height: 6⅛ inches. Private collection, New York City.

Plate 66   Vase, c. 1895–1900. Height: 7⅝ inches. Private collection, New York City.

Plate 67
Vase, c. 1895–1900.
Height: 5⅜ inches. Private collection, New York City.

Plate 68
Vase, c. 1895–1900.
Height: 5½ inches. Private collection, New York City.

Plate 69
Bowl with snakes, c. 1895–1900.
Height: 5⅛ inches. Private collection, New York City.

Plate 70   Vase, c. 1898–1907. Height: 7¾ inches. Private collection, New York City.

Plate 71   Vase, c. 1900. Height: 9½ inches. Andrew Van Styn, Chicago.

Plate 72
Vase, c. 1898.
Height: 7⅞ inches. Private collection, New York City.

Plate 73
Vase, c. 1895–1900.
Height: 4¾ inches. Private collection, New York City.

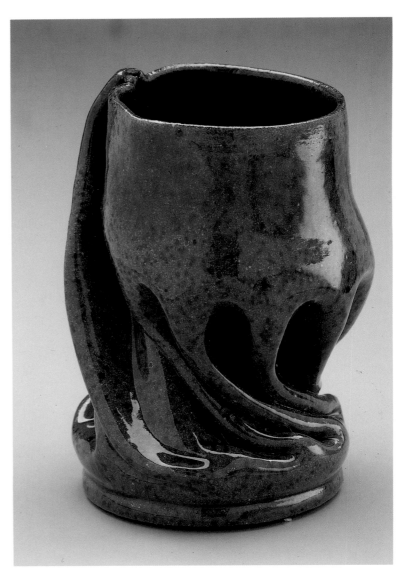

Plate 74
Vase, c. 1895–1900.
Height: 3⅜ inches. Private collection, New York.

Plate 75
Vase, c. 1895–1900.
Height: 7½ inches. Private collection, New York City.

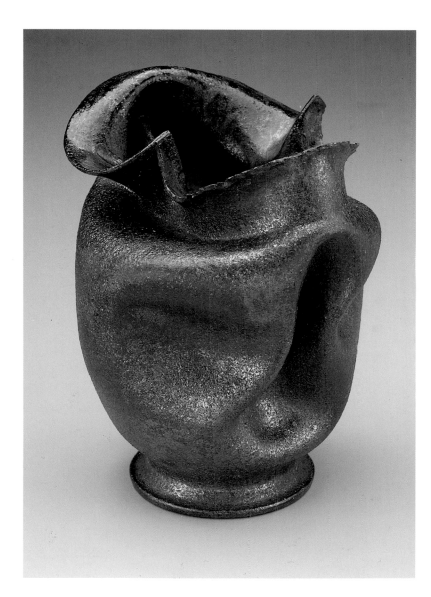

Plate 76
Vase, c. 1895–1900.
Height: 5⅝ inches. Private collection, New York City.

Plate 77
Vase, c. 1895–1900.
Height: 6½ inches. Private collection, New York City.

Plate 78
Vase, c. 1902–7.
Height: 5¾ inches. Private collection, New York City.

Plate 79
Bowl, c. 1902–7.
Height: 4¼ inches. Andrew Van Styn, Chicago.

Plate 80
Vase, c. 1902–7.
Height: 5 inches. Private collection, New York City.

Plate 81   Vase, c. 1895–1900. Height: 9 inches. Private collection. New York City.

Plate 82
Bowl, c. 1902–7.
Height: 4¾ inches.
Andrew Van Styn, Chicago.

Plate 83
Bowl, c. 1902–7.
Height: 4½ inches. Private collection,
New York City.

Plate 84
Small bowl, c. 1895–1900.
Height: 4 inches. Private collection,
Montague, New Jersey.

Plate 85
Small bowl, c. 1898–1907
Height: 4 inches.
Private collection,
New York City.

Plate 86
Vase, c. 1895–1900.
Height: 6 inches.
Andrew Van Styn, Chicago.

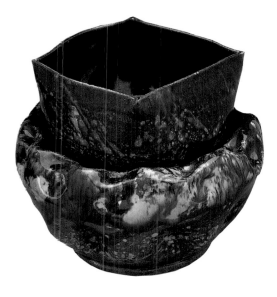

Plate 87
Bowl, c. 1895–1900.
Height: 5 inches. Private collection,
New York City.

Plate 88
Bowl, c. 1895–1900.
Height: 4¼ inches.
Private collection,
Montague, New Jersey.

Plate 89   Footed bowl, c. 1895–1900. Height: 7½ inches. Private collection, New York City.

I am making pots for art sake, God sake, the future generation and — by present indications — for my own satisfaction, but when I'm gone (like Palissy), my work will be prized, honored and cherished.

George Edgar Ohr, 1899.

In 1968 James W. Carpenter, an antiques dealer from New Jersey, was traveling through Biloxi, Mississippi, in search of veteran automobiles. He had heard about the Ohr Boys' Auto Repair Shop, and, hoping to find an early Cadillac or perhaps a Model T Ford, he contacted the surviving Ohr children to arrange a visit. When he met them at the family warehouse he was greeted not by classic cars but by a collection of over seven thousand of the strangest and most wonderful pots he had ever seen, all crafted by George Ohr, a potter then obscure in the ranks of American ceramists. Reluctant to sell his wares to an unappreciative public, Ohr had hoarded almost his entire mature output, predicting that it would be "purchased by the entire nation,"[1] which would then erect a temple to his genius. What Carpenter found gave evidence of a talent of greater power and sophistication than anyone had imagined.

It took two years of negotiations and a reported fifty thousand dollars to acquire this cache of pots. In 1972 Carpenter made the works available for purchase in an antiques store in a small New Jersey town and commissioned Robert Blasberg to write a monograph about the eccentric potter. This reappearance by Ohr was not as he had predicted. But then Carpenter was not in the business of building temples. Still, his return could not have been more dramatic—or more controversial—had the master potter/showman orchestrated it himself. Historians of the Arts and Crafts Movement were suddenly forced to reevaluate Ohr's importance. Art pottery collectors were startled and intrigued by the "new" work. And New York City's contemporary art world discovered Ohr, conferring on him the status of cult figure. Ohr had indeed returned, as he had predicted he would, to be evaluated by a future generation. His timing, for once, was perfect.

As with all prophets Ohr is difficult to appraise. It is always arguable whether the vision of such artists is simply a coincidence, a chronological anomaly, or whether they owe their prescience to their courage in venturing out onto the avant-garde edge. We may ponder these distinctions, but Ohr never doubted his role. He knew that he was dealing in a new intensity of expression. He was also all too aware that he would probably never receive the recognition that he so ardently desired.

The precise reasons for the abrupt end of Ohr's career as a potter (around 1907) are not known. He may have decided that he had achieved what he had been placed on earth to do, or perhaps having his art go unappreciated for so long had simply become too frustrating. So Ohr turned his back on the world of art and busied himself by assisting his sons in running their repair shop until his death in 1918.

His obituary in the Biloxi *Daily Herald* declared him to be "Celebrated throughout the United States as a Fashioner of Pottery."[2] This was kind but inaccurate. Once the Mad Potter of Biloxi had removed himself from the ceramic arts arena, his brief flirtation with celebrity (or notoriety) came to an end. Long before Ohr died he was already forgotten. After his death an attempt was made to sell his pots, but without success.[3] Practically unknown by the mid-

Clay Prophet: A Present Day Appraisal

BY GARTH CLARK

Figure 91
Ohr's pots in the family warehouse in Biloxi, c. 1968–69.

1920s, Ohr's hoard of pots was thrown into boxes and set aside in the family warehouse. In the years that followed, his talent was judged by only a handful of pots, mostly minor works in private and public collections. From this meager evidence he was rated as a skilled if eccentric potter but not an artist of consequence. As late as 1972 the few works in known collections were considered to be his total extant ouevre.[4]

Ohr appears to have anticipated many developments we now take for granted in contemporary art, particularly in ceramics. In the words of critic John Coplans, he was "a pre-Dada Dadaist and a pre-Surrealism Surrealist."[5] His approach to materials and to wheel-thrown manipulations was not equalled, or even attempted, in the ceramics world until the mid-1950s. Ohr also fashioned imagery, verbal-visual plays, and scatalogical references that were central concerns of the Funk ceramists of the 1960s. Ohr's vessels are imbued with a complexity of both formal visual concerns and symbolic issues. These modestly scaled vessels contain a spirit of heroic proportions—a spirit that is moving for its ambition and courage.

To get under the skin of Ohr's pots and their maker, this essay approaches his art from a highly personal point of view, examining its influences and its connections to other art—what George Kubler refers to as "linked solutions."[6] By the nature of Ohr's prophecy, these "linked solutions" occur more frequently in our lifetime than they did in his. While this process may well be speculative, it is also highly revealing. This short and unlikely list of concerns central to Ohr's art provides a structure for this inquiry: God, Sex, The Wheel, Drawing, Color, Language, and Ohr the Clown. Together these motifs give shape to Ohr's creative psyche.

Figure 92
Ohr playing the role of Moses, c. 1908.

Ohr and/as God

Ay, note that potter's wheel,
That metaphor! and feel
Why time spins fast, why passive lies our clay,—
Thou to whom fools propound

When the wine makes its round
'Since life fleets, all is change; the Past gone,
*   seize today!'*

Fool! All that is, at all,
Lasts ever, past recall;
Earth changes, but thy soul and God stand
sure:
What entered into thee,
Time was, is, and shall be:
Time's wheel runs back or stops; Potter and Clay
*   endure.*

Robert Browning, "Rabbi Ben Ezra"

The tradition of theomorphism—giving god-like symbolism to acts or objects—has long been linked with pottery. In the culture of the prehistoric Mimbres Indians, a dead man's pots were punctured so that his soul could escape to nirvana. Frescoes in ancient Egyptian tombs show man being created by the gods on the potter's wheel, and the Bible eloquently echoes that creationist metaphor: "O Lord, thou art our father; we are the clay, and thou our potter; and we all are the work of your hand" (Isaiah 64:8).

One who "never missed a literary dab on ceramics,"[7] Ohr was greatly influenced by the Bible's verses describing the potter and his clay and also by the poetry of Robert Browning and Omar Khayyám. The latter had a particularly strong impact on Ohr, who humorously took on the title of "Biloxies Ohrmer Kayam." But for all his punning, Ohr was deeply moved by Khayyám's *Rubáiyát,* and in particular, by the following passage:

None answered this; but after Silence spake
A Vessel of a more ungainly Make;
*   "They Sneer at me for leaning all awry;*
What! did the Hand then of the Potter shake?"

Ohr's obsessive commitment to the theomorphic role of the potter as the giver of life infused his art with a spiritual intensity and grace. Yet Ohr was not a religious man in the conventional sense. He did not accept God as a dictator of everyday morality. He was not above sacrilegious humor or acts. And he viewed the church with the same mistrust he accorded all institutions of the establishment. But he was, according to his pronouncements, a confirmed adherent of theism, the belief in God as the creative source of man, whose transcendent spirit is immanent in the world.

This belief prompted Ohr's motto, "no two pieces alike!" But Ohr's contemporary critics, such as the pottery designer Frederick Hurten Rhead, misinterpreted this insistence on individuality as the act of a show-off. "He deliberately distorted every pot he made in order to be violently different from any other potter," Rhead complained.[8] But Ohr was simply obeying a deep belief in the uniqueness of man. "I am the apostle of individuality," he said, "the brother of the human race . . . but I must be myself and want every pot to be itself."[9]

Ohr spoke of his pots as "mud babies" and confessed: "I brood over [each pot] with the same tenderness a mortal child awakens in its parent."[10] He spread his affection equally, treating his "ungainly" pots with as much love as those that were more handsome.[11] After much of his pottery was destroyed by fire in 1894 he carefully assembled the remains of the broken and charred pots, placed them in boxes, and kept them in the backyard, referring to them with macabre tenderness as his "killed babies." Asked by an interviewer why he did not throw these away, Ohr replied, "Did you ever hear of a mother so inhuman that she would cast off her deformed child?"[12]

While at times Ohr appeared to be merely God's apostle, as he claimed, more often one senses that he took on the role of the Godhead—the creator of individual souls contained in his fragile clay vessels. In some ways this attitude may seem unduly eccentric, but it has a touching, poignant quality, a direct and almost primeval response to creativity and to the sanctity of individuality and the human spirit.

This spiritual fervor succored Ohr through the paternalism and sarcasm of critics and the disappointing and painful dismissal of his talent by the art world at large. He approached his pottery-making as a theistic mission. And yet despite his passionate belief in God as the creative force, he never became a zealot. His faith was balanced by an open, sensual approach to

life, a wicked sense of humor, and by all accounts, a highly developed libido.

The Sexual Ohr

[Ohr] couldn't keep his hands off the tactile body of his forms. The curvaceous profiles beckoned and he succumbed. He literalized the erotic skin of the vessel's surface: every spout a sexualized orifice, every handle designed for fondling, every asymmetry slouches toward indolent lovemaking.

Jeff Perrone, Arts Magazine, *1985.*

Ohr's interest in eroticism found two distinct lines of expression in his pottery. Playful, sexist, and vulgar, the first took shape in his lewd country-fair gimcracks (which Hecht so delightfully terms *bawdywares*). The second was abstract, sensual, and powerfully moving, and was incorporated into his art pots. The latter contributed to Ohr's serious art, while

or "You have a fine pair of balls." He also created money banks whose fronts were detailed vaginas with incised pubic hair and whose backs resembled breasts. These crude pieces were manufactured to raise sniggers—and dollars—at country fairs. There were neither ironies nor transformations within these objects to make them anything more than novelties. Interestingly enough, however, they do have something in common with a later development in American ceramics, the so-called Funk movement.[13]

Led by Robert Arneson in the 1960s, Funk ceramists explored an offensive, scatalogical, and visceral content in works whose imagery was cast in the same vulgar manner as those of the country-fair gimcrack-maker. In *Telephone* (1965), for example, Arneson produced a telephone with a vagina for an earpiece and a penis for a receiver. The Funk movement reveled in coarse, lowbrow humor as a deliberate means of shocking the viewer. But one should be cautious in using the ceramics of the Funk movement to legitimize Ohr's bawdryness. Its goal was to make a consciously anti-art statement by deliberately attacking the status quo. Ohr's goal was simply entertainment and profit.

Ohr's art pots reveal the serious side of his eroticism, thinly disguised through abstraction to pass inspection. One of the less innocent of the works, however, is a pot in the collection of Patti Zanone (Plate 111). The pot's top section is essentially a vagina reposing atop a cylinder that is twisted two-thirds of the way up its height to resemble a phallus. Glazed a pinkish red, the lips on the piece droop across the cylinder with a languid eroticism, giving the appearance of being swollen and aroused. While the piece's imagery is explicit, it is nonetheless also ambiguous, with the phallus playing the role of the womb.

The pot is unusual in that Ohr was rarely so literal in exploring sexuality in his work. Nonetheless the vessel is quite successful in its marriage of taught, modern form and powerful eroticism, and it carries much the same presence as Brancusi's *Princess* (1916), a bronze sculpture of male genitals elegantly reduced to their sculptural (and anatomical) essence. Ohr's

Figure 95
Above, set of brothel tokens in press-molded earthenware. Ohr sold trinkets of this kind at county and state fairs and as souvenirs to Biloxi's visitors. Private collection, New York.

Figure 96
Right, Georgia O'Keeffe, *Black Iris*, 1926. The Metropolitan Museum of Art, New York; The Alfred Stieglitz Collection, 1949.

Opposite page:

Figure 97
Robert Arneson, *Telephone*, 1965. Private collection, Princeton, New Jersey.

Figure 98
Small vase by Ohr from around 1900 (see Plate 111).

Figure 99
Constantin Brancusi, *Princess X*, 1916. Philadelphia Museum of Art; Louise and Walter Arensberg Collection.

the former played to the commercial side of his exhibitionism and pandered to his Rabelaisian front as a horny, macho blacksmith-potter.

Ohr made brothel tokens inscribed with words, phonetic sounds, and images that composed such bawdy messages as "I owe you one screw"

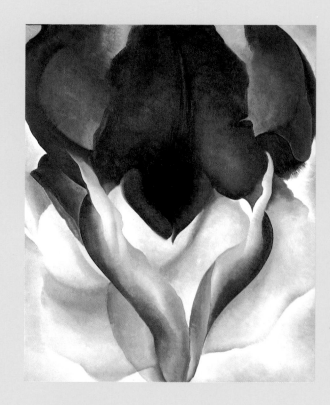

"vagina" pot is, despite its modest scale (just over six and a half inches high), unquestionably one of his masterworks.

The pot is also unusual in that it shows both a male and female form. Given Ohr's keen interest in the sexual, it is surprising how infrequently he used the male organ as a symbol or metaphor in his work. He did produce some phallic forms, but most were made in jest. Hecht has already described the presentation of one of these pieces to a local magistrate. In another pot Ohr has drawn the penis within a camouflage of leaves and foliage. But again this was Ohr playing games. Among his art pots there are only a few phallic forms. One finds bullet-shaped vessels in a group of unusually severe, gun-metal-glazed pots, but these are rare and atypical works.

On close inspection Ohr's pots are not what one would expect of a burly blacksmith-potter. The editor of *Brick* magazine raised this point when he praised Ohr's pots as being "the daintiest and most delicate."[14] When one observes carefully, one finds that Ohr's vessels do not celebrate the male yang but are rather a deeply felt homage to the feminine ying. The forms are invariably gentle and enclosing. The mouths of his pots metamorphose into soft, ruffled vulvas. The volumes become wombs.

Ohr confirms this symbolism. "Each piece of pottery I make is a baby," he said on many occasions.[15] What is curious, and most revealing, is that Ohr consistently presented himself as the mother of his clay babies. He was the giver of birth. This puts Ohr's eroticism into a revealing context. His interest in sex was not prurient, as expressed in his art pots, but derived from an obsession with fecundity that in turn was connected with his theist beliefs. Ohr saw birth, sexuality, and God as the source of all creative expression. So committed was he to this notion that in his pottery he set aside the male sexual ethos and took on the so-called dark principle of the feminine ying.

Of the early modernists' work painter Georgia O'Keeffe's calla lilies and other flowers undulate with the same lyricism and enclosing sexuality as do Ohr's pots (although she insisted that her

work is not about vaginas). They reveal the same fragility, ruffled orifices, sense of containment—and hint of secret spaces. The two artists also share a tenderness in their handling of this content.

Yet Ohr's pots go beyond a sensual exploration of the female form, in a balance between eroticism and wit reminiscent of Marcel Duchamp's readymade *Fig Leaf* (1951).[16] Indeed Ohr's pots would find themselves in harmony with many of the erotic works of the early Dada and Surrealist artists. His pots could happily stand alongside Man Ray's photography or Hans Bellmer's sculptures, with their almost febrile fascination with the female anatomy and their undertow of fetishism.

The Dada and Surrealist objects exude a strong sense of the fetish, what *Webster's Dictionary* defines (with an uncharacteristic touch of drama) as a "pathological displacement of erotic interest" towards a sexualized object, shape, or form. It is true of the fetish that its erotic fascination can be greatest when the fetish is most abstract, merely suggesting sexual content, as we see in Man Ray's erotic photographs. His images that allude to women's sexual body parts are, in fact, quite innocent. Yet the sexual fascination unleashed by the forms in the photographs is made all the more suggestive by their imaginative abstraction.

The same is true of Ohr's pots: their expression of sexuality is often experienced most deliciously where the eroticism is most subtle. Some pots do no more than suggest— unspecifically—a fold of flesh. Like a brief glimpse of a thigh beneath a skirt, the pots give access to moments of intimacy through private, forbidden anthropomorphism. Ohr's pots, in common with the man who made them, are sexual entities.

Ohr and the Wheel

It is said that Ohr could work on the wheel whichever way it turned. Certainly he could throw wares of considerable size with walls much thinner than any other potter ever has

Figure 100
Ohr working at the potter's wheel, 1890s. Proud of his blacksmith's strength, Ohr reputedly had a cast made of his arm for the drawing class at Newcomb College.

Figure 101
Peter Voulkos, *Rocking Pot*, 1957. Private collection, Princeton, New Jersey.

accomplished. It is quite probable that George Ohr, rated simply as a mechanic, was the most expert thrower that the craft has ever known.

Paul E. Cox, Ceramic Age, *1935.*

The potter's wheel was the generator of energy in Ohr's art. Apart from its theomorphic connotations, its ability to employ centrifugal force to create form was, for Ohr, a magical process. "When I first found the wheel," he wrote in a wonderfully poetic expression of his passion for this machine, "I felt it all over like a wild duck in water."[17] In an interview in 1901 he expanded upon this, saying that "when I looked at the first [potter's wheel], I knew I was home. . . . Since then I have built many castles in the air, but they have all been of clay."[18]

Ohr was exceedingly proud of his prowess at the wheel and ever ready to demonstrate his skills to the visitors who came to his workshop

or to larger audiences at state and county fairs. Never one to hide behind false modesty, Ohr described his technical wizardry: "This is what I [can] do, with four pounds of clay on the wheel—blindfolded—turn a jug, put a corncob stopper in it, change the corncob into a funnell, have the funnell disappear, and have a jar, change the jar into an urn and half a dozen other shapes and turn anything that anyone in the U.S.A. can mention that is syndrical on that potters wheel."[19]

Ohr was extraordinarily skilled at the wheel, but skill is common enough in the history of ceramics. What set him apart was what he *did* with his skills. Ohr used the wheel to release and/or contain energies, creating pots more radical than anything else produced during his time. He whirled off into a new aesthetic, pushing his "twisted, crinkled conglomerations" to the point of collapse. He also used throwing to express content. Ohr never spoke of "good design" or even "good form." He was seeking communion with his ideas and spirit, reaching out for his unique emotional matrix. "Shapes come to a potter as verses to the poet," he was fond of saying. "Clay follows the fingers and the fingers follow the mind."[20]

There is a curiously similar refrain in the words of Peter Voulkos, the so-called Abstract Expressionist potter whose work revolutionized the form and role of the vessel in contemporary American art. "When you touch clay it moves," says Voulkos, "you must learn to dance with it."[21] The changes in the vocabulary of the vessel that Voulkos and his students introduced in the late 1950s created a highly sympathetic climate for Ohr's return, and a comparison of the two is instructive.

In common with Ohr, Voulkos was an exceptional thrower. Voulkos began as a maker of functional wares, but in the mid-fifties, after he established a ceramics department at the Otis Art Institute in Los Angeles, his work began to change.[22] Together with a group of gifted students Voulkos began to explore the vessel in a nontraditionalist, nonformalist, nonutilitarian manner. He created large pots on the wheel that were then vigorously altered into powerful, deeply scored asymmetrical forms.

The first public debate over his work came in 1961 when Rose Slivka published an article in *Craft Horizons* entitled "The New Ceramic Presence," which dealt with and illustrated works by Voulkos and Co.[23] The response from the membership of the American Craft Council, the publisher of the magazine, was one of outrage, confusion, and dismay. Letters to the editor assailed Voulkos's pots as "deformed" and "mutilated," much the same criticisms that had been leveled against Ohr's work. But the times were different for Voulkos. Within a decade the condemnation had changed into adulation and Voulkos was accepted as an important American artist. He and the artists who gathered around him—Ken Price, Jerry Rothman, Ron Nagle, Jim Melchert, John Mason, Paul Soldner, and others—transformed the vessel into a potent format for expressing the ideas of abstract art, and in the process they greatly increased the ceramic literacy of the American art-viewing public and their institutions.

Voulkos's work received broad acceptance because Abstract Expressionist painting had transfigured the way Americans viewed abstract art. It validated the notion of happenstance, of gestural energy, and of trusting the hand and materials to find solutions. This was what critic Harold Rosenberg had labelled "action art," with its accent upon the physical and the intuitive.

Ohr's treatment of his forms showed a fierce commitment to the same aesthetic of risk that motivated Voulkos: when the pot stood glistening, wet, and symmetrical on the wheel, it was ready to be altered. The ultimate character of the work of the two potters, however, was markedly different. Voulkos's pots were unequivocally masculine, with an emphasis on vertical, thrusting forms. Their diminished sense of volume accentuated their mass and the sculptural power of the work. The surface treatment was summary, direct, and raw.

Whereas volume dominated Ohr's thin-walled, paper-light pots, their sense of mass was negligible. Labeled as grotesque in his day, these pots can now be seen as a tour de force of delicacy and restraint. Ohr's range of surface manipulations was much more complex and varied than Voulkos's and often resulted in a total reshaping of the original form. The method that Ohr employed—pummeling, twisting, or folding—was not innovative in itself. (Ruffling, for instance, was a popular and common technique in Victorian glass.) The technique originated long before the Arts and Crafts Movement, as can be seen from an example of a sixth-century proto-Yueh funerary urn (compare Figures 102, 103). Again what set Ohr apart was what he *did* with his skills. Dismissing the more effete and decorative work that abounded in his day, Ohr was furiously gestural with his forms. His manipulations of the clay were extreme, almost shockingly alive with movement.

Some pieces swayed to the most regular of rhythms, as evenly spaced pleats collapsed about the shoulder of a pot or dissected the neck of a vase. Indeed, despite the unusual appearance of the work, the term classical comes to mind. But most interesting are those where the *entire* pot is caught in the thrall of linear motion (Plates 74, 93, 116, 121). Here movement encompasses the entire form. The pot breaks down into a series of related but independent volumes, transforming the work into a kinesthetic labyrinth while still retaining an overall sense of unity and composition.

What further enobles these forms is the lightness, or more accurately, the *deftness*, of Ohr's touch. The pots succeed visually because they appear almost accidental. Allowing the forms to find their own way, Ohr seems only to have given a nudge here or a tuck there—the rest of the movement has the inevitability of an organic process. No doubt Ohr's control was much more deliberate and exacting than is revealed, and the skill necessary to produce these works was considerable, but it is the *illusion* of effortlessness that makes great pots. As the Japanese potter Hamada would insist, a good pot should arrive without any obvious sense of effort, "like a man walking downhill in a cool breeze."[24]

The purpose of Ohr's craftsmanship was greatly misunderstood in his day. Art had not yet arrived at the post-Craft phase of the 1920s that regarded technique in more casual and metaphysical terms. The dominant aesthetic force for a potter in Ohr's day came from the Arts and Crafts Movement, which valued fine craftsmanship above creativity. The potter Adelaide Alsop Robineau is a case in point. Her pots were highly derivative and almost totally devoid of modern concerns or influences. Except for a few masterpieces, most were ostentatiously overworked and overcrafted. Her craftsmanship, however, was exceptional, and for this reason her work was greatly admired and honored within the movement.[25]

No doubt Ethel Hutson believed she was bestowing a rare accolade on Ohr when she commented, in 1905, on the value of handcrafted work. "So it is that George Ohr, with all his extravagant claims and grotesque eccentricities, is doing good work, if he opens the eyes of even a few people to the truth that a piece of handmade pottery is valuable as a piece of craftsmanship, in the same way that a piece of hand-embroidery, or hand wrought metal is esteemed above the product of the loom or the foundry."[26]

Ohr's view of his craft could not have been further from Hutson's. Her idealized vision of the craftsman required a distance from the hard realities of a *true* craftsman's life, something akin to Marie Antoinette playing shepherdess. Nor did Robineau confront the daily toil of running a small-town pottery. While she was wonderfully skilled, with a lifetime production of merely six hundred pots she (and her ilk) could afford to have a romantic perspective on her craft. Indeed most of the so-called potters of the movement, William Grueby, Mary Chase Perry, and others, were potters only in the white-collar sense of being glaze chemists and designers. They worked in small factories where all the drudgery of craft was assumed by poorly paid workers.

Ohr *was* a romantic, but not about his craft. He was born into an artisan's family. His father was a blacksmith and Ohr spent much of his youth unhappily helping out in the workshop. It was difficult for one born into the utilitarian craft world to feel the same "romance" for this heritage as those from middle-class backgrounds who chose, often with the benefit of private incomes, to take on the mantle of craftsman. Ohr made it clear that he did not view his production of thousands of flower pots and pitchers for Biloxi's housewives as preserving a tradition—it was simply a means of paying his way—and he treated these customers with an indifference verging on rudeness.

It must be remembered that Ohr worked under the constant threat of financial collapse. He could not afford to take on many assistants. To save money he even dug his own clay. His son Oto recalls Ohr's trips across the river, with

Figure 102
The ruffling we see on this sixth-century proto-Yueh funerary urn from China is something that occurs throughout the history of ceramics, in various cultures and over thousands of years. The ruffling can be achieved on the wheel or by working from applied coils of clay. Nelson-Atkins Museum of Art, Kansas City; Gift of Mrs. W. R. McCormack.

Figure 103
Compare the ruffling in Figure 102 with this piece by Ohr, which dramatically illustrates how eccentric and extreme is his exploration of this technique. (See Plate 92.)

horse and wagon, to gather clay. It would take three days for Ohr, single-handedly, to dig the clay and return to the pottery. Then began the arduous process of cleaning and preparing the clay in a concrete pit.[27] This was not the stuff of romance.

What Ohr was passionate about was art, what he could entice out of the clay's plasticity. The conceptual purpose of Ohr's pottery—a commitment to individuality—overrode the craftsmanship. The ruffling, twisting, pummeling, tearing, folding, and pinching was meant to imbue each pot with its own personality. He was investing his pots with the same uniqueness that he believed God gave to souls. This distortion of the sanctity of the vessel, what his peers saw as wanton acts of destruction, was paradoxically what vitalized his clay babies. His surface handling was the symbolic equivalent of a midwife's smacking the buttocks of a newborn child, encouraging it to draw its first breath. Decades later Jean Cocteau drew a comparison with the ceramic doves and female figures that Picasso had fashioned by taking thrown forms and twisting them into bird and human shapes, saying to Picasso, "you wring their necks and give them life."[28]

How Ohr worked his pots into unconventional forms is familiar to almost every apprentice potter. The pleating and collapsing of the ceramic forms occurs by accident (albeit without any of Ohr's lyricism and grace) when the centrifugal force from the wheel is applied off center and the potter loses control. In a sense, Ohr was returning to his very first weeks at the wheel and drawing on the potential of this period of innocence and discovery. As critic Jeff Perrone explains, "Ohr toyed with ceramic form like no one before him, and the beauty is that he was only doing those things people do when they first fool around with clay: they play. The difference? People push unstructured lumps around in order to discover the potentials; Ohr played with perfect pots as his raw materials, 'making' them by destroying their perfection, their ideal symmetries. He began where ceramists before him ended, and began/ ended where the novice begins."[29] This urge to "deconstruct" his forms helps to animate Ohr's pots. While his pots frequently achieve the sub-

lime, this does not appear to be Ohr's goal. The purpose of the deconstructive process is more edgy, more concerned with uncovering ambiguity and contradiction than achieving reductive purity.

Drawing

The balance of the spout and handle of a teapot, with each other and with the body of the pot, is an aesthetic problem to which no artist need be ashamed to devote his attention. There is not only the problem of balancing two linear [elements], each with a distinct function, against each other, but these forms must both accord with the three dimensional volume of the body of the pot. The correct solution to this problem is one of the rarest of aesthetic achievements.

Herbert Read, Art and Industry, *1936.*

For a potter the most dynamic means of drawing is not by making sketches or patterns on a pot's surface but by attaching handles, spouts,

Figure 104
Ohr preparing his clay, which he dug himself during three-day expeditions with horse and cart. Here we see Harry Portman in the background, sometime around 1896 or 1897. The horse on the left powers the mulling well that grinds the clay.

and other linear appendages to the pottery forms. This arrangement is complex because the linear attachments, as Read points out, must work in juxtaposition to the volumes to which they are attached. Ohr was a superb draftsman whose masterful handles were both functional and dramatic.

Ohr did not randomly assign handles to pots but deliberately threw and assembled certain forms specifically for this purpose. The "function" of his handles, to give a visual unity to an assembly of otherwise disparate forms, is easily appreciated by simply blocking the handles from view on some of the illustrations of his pots in this book. The "de-handled" forms that remain appear incomplete and anemic.

Ohr used several kinds of handles on his pots; some were molded and others carved. But primarily he produced tendril-like handles from ribbons of plastic clay. These he "drew" in space with the skill of a calligrapher, mimicking the liquid sense of line on the host volume. The handles superficially resemble the style of art nouveau. However, given the fact that these handles started to appear around 1896, when the organic, whiplash art nouveau was just beginning to take root in Paris and Belgium, it is likely that Ohr's line sprang from the organic qualities of the clay itself. One feels compelled

to concur with Marion John Nelson that while the handles are "highly suggestive of European art nouveau . . . the similarity is apparently co-incidental."[30] More probably the curvilinear aspect of the handles derived from Ohr's experience as a blacksmith, when he would have worked with ornamental wrought iron. The similarity in style and handling seems to be more than accidental given his intimate knowledge of this medium.

In his teapots Ohr used molded handles, placing them more with regard to their use as a visual counterpart to the main volume than with any real concern for their utilitarian efficiency. Spouts were used in much the same way as the handles. Ohr would lengthen or shorten the spouts to fit the shape of the main form and to provide contrapuntal balance with the handles attached to the other end.

One of the most stunning of these teapots, in the Shack collection, is a large, black vessel with the most superbly drawn handle and spout that enclose the rotund main form with fluid *élan* (Figure 105). It is doubtful that these teapots were made to serve tea, for in some cases Ohr deliberately satirized their function. One of the finest visual puns is captured in a monumental and masterful teapot in the collection of the National Museum of History and Technology of the Smithsonian Institution. This dual coffeepot/teapot is a witty assemblage of lids, handles, and spouts, glazed black on one side and green on the other (Figure 106). Presumably it could function, but its primary impact is visual.

Ohr also attached to the vessel anywhere from three to five differently shaped handles. The intent—and effect—was, again, a humorous comment upon the nature of the vessel and its traditions. Ohr also had another purpose: to cause confusion about the function of the handle and subvert its traditional role to that of a sculptural or decorative device. On the surface these wares are simple jokes, but the way the handles and forms are composed is so canny and inventive that these pieces take on a strong sculptural/linear presence and more than a touch of ironic self-examination.

Figure 105
Ohr teapot, c. 1900. Private collection, New York.

The one flat note in Ohr's surface appendages is his use of the serpent. While Ohr's pots with serpents fetch handsome prices, one can only assume that the value placed on these pieces corresponds to their rarity. Ohr's reason for adding the serpents is difficult to fathom, but it could have originated from his identification with Bernard Palissy and his wares.

On occasional pots, usually those that are extremely unconventional in form, the serpents can work superbly (Plates 63, 104). Generally, however, these loutish worms tend to distract and disfigure. Their summary modeling seems all the more crude when compared to the elegance of the forms they adorn. They often destroy the composition of a form without compensating by setting up an interesting polarization of contrasts. They are one of the few truly perverse products of an otherwise remarkably intuitive eye.

Ohr and Color

Colors and Quality counts nothing in my creations. . . . God, put no color or quality in souls.

George Edgar Ohr, c. 1900.

Ohr angrily scrawled these words in his spidery hand around the border of a photograph of unglazed pots, his response to the critics who simply could not come to terms with his forms. Most shared the view of the distinguished ceramics historian Edwin Atlee Barber that "the principal beauty of the ware consists in the richness of the glazes, which are wonderfully varied."[31]

None of the important writers on ceramics (with the exception of the loyal William King) endorsed Ohr's forms, and even King said that Ohr's clay must "cry out in anguish and anger against such desecration."[32] Charles Fergus Binns, director of the New York School of Clayworking and Ceramics at Alfred University, used Ohr's forms as an example to his students of facility gone haywire. Ethel Hutson's

comment in the *Clay Worker* was typical of the criticism leveled at Ohr: "Mr. Ohr suffers from his efforts to make it original at any cost of beauty and aesthetic charm. Often ingenious, and always unusual, as his work is, it is the lack of good proportion, of grace and of dignity that makes it fail to produce on the spectator the effect a work of art should produce. One is reminded of those grotesque and rugged poems

Figure 106
Ohr teapot and coffeepot, c. 1900. Glazed black on one side and mottled green-yellow on the other. National Museum of History and Technology, The Smithsonian Institution, Washington, D.C.; Gift of James W. Carpenter.

Figure 107
A selection of Biloxi bisque ware with Ohr's words scrawled around the border.

of Robert Browning's, which even his most ardent admirers cannot defend; so perversely do they offend the ear and the sense of euphony."[33]

The English ceramist Michael Cardew always contended that the success of any pot was determined ninety-five percent by its form and that no quantity of glaze or decoration could rescue a poor form from ignominy. Ohr believed this as well. Glazing his pots was patently a secondary concern for him, although he showed genius both as a colorist and a chemist.

It is understandable that Ohr's contemporaries were seduced by his polychromatic pyrotechnics. Ohr's glazes are remarkable. They have the verve and finesse of Eastern ceramics, in particular, the three-color Tang wares and the rich, saturated color of Japan's Momoyama and Oribe wares. They also resemble the pal-

ettes of Palissy and of the low-fire pottery of eighteenth-century Staffordshire ceramics. The inspiration for Ohr's glazes is a matter of speculation and is ultimately unimportant. What matters is that we understand his view that his glazes were the servants of his forms, not their *raison d'être*.

There is a tendency, particularly among collectors of art pottery, to fall into Barber's trap and overvalue the quality of an Ohr piece based on its glaze, a situation reflected in the high prices received in auction for unusually glazed pots (no matter how ordinary the form they may clothe). For the marketplace, at least, the "principal value" of the pots remains in the glaze. This bias has led to the regrettable practice of glazing bisqued pots (known to Ohr collectors by the misnomer of "reglazed" pots) and selling them as genuine Ohr surfaces.

Ohr's highly colored glazes are not always successful. In some pots the wash of histrionic, multihued surfaces tends to overwhelm the form, distort its line, and blur its kinesthetic energies. The more dramatic glazes require an intelligent symbiosis between surface and form. Happily this union occurred frequently; a fine example is the pummeled bowl (Plate 108), where the dappled color works energetically with the relief surface, setting up a push/pull resonance between positive and negative space. In some cases, however, the use of the standard clear glaze is more appropriate. A small vase in the collection of Irving Blum, for instance, draws its power and strength from its simplicity and the directness of its line (Plate 113). A multicolored glaze would have diminished the impact and economy of this remarkable form.

Ohr's attitude about color has also given his unglazed pots a new status. These were previously considered to be pots that did not make the trip to the glaze bucket. Now it is appreciated that he intended many of the bisque pots to remain unglazed. Many of the best of these have been destroyed by the greed of the "reglazers."

Some exceptional examples of Ohr's bisqued pots have survived. A notable example is the monumental vase in the Tanner collection. But equally impressive in their eccentric vitality

Figure 108
A major unglazed earthenware urn by Ohr, c. 1906. This is one of Ohr's most elaborate bisque pieces, on which he has inscribed the words "Mary had a little lamb and George has a little pot-ohr-e." Robert Tannen, New Orleans.

are Ohr's small unglazed, agateware bowls believed to be his last series of work. These virtuoso pieces, among his most extreme manipulations, have a tougher edge than most of his work, and their lyricism is often fractured by seemingly disruptive moments. The surfaces are not without color: the clay combinations vary from light buff and orange to dark brown and black/grey. The undulating waves of contrasting earth tones float across the pots in harmony with the manipulations of the surface. The dull surfaces absorb, rather than reflect, light and the ruffles, folds, and indentations create a moody chiaroscuro quite different in character to that of the glazed pots—somber, meditative, and inward. Here and there is a flash of anger in the sudden fractures that punctuate the forms—protests, perhaps, of a deeply personal nature made at a time when Ohr was planning to give up his beloved wheel. Whatever these pots mean to say, they act as a reminder to keep the seduction of glazes at arm's length.

Ohr and Language

We are of the opinion that Mr. Ohr has missed his calling. Literature is the thing for him. In the formation of his literary style Mr. Ohr has evidently drunk deep at many founts, but if we judge right, at none so deeply as Browning's dark, esoteric manner.

A New York newspaper, 1898.

The fact that a handbill written by Ohr could elicit such a lengthy retort from a New York newspaper is quite a tribute to the energy and provocative quality of Ohr's writing, and it raises the issue of the relationship between language and Ohr's art—and more broadly the changing role of language as part of the environment of the visual artist. In 1898 language was just starting to merge with the visual arts. The symbolist poets and painters in Paris had already begun an exchange of energy and ideas. Then the Futurists, the Dadaists, and later the Surrealists began to incorporate language into their art and started to write and aggressively present manifestos, performances, and poetry that expanded upon the visual ideas in their

work. Painters began to include onomatopoetic words in their paintings. In the late 1910s assemblage artists such as Kurt Schwitters and Johannes Baader converted text into a raw material with which to create contextual form. Since then contemporary artists from Ed Ruscha to Barbara Kruger and Jenny Holzer have moved language into a "visual" genre that is now as established as the landscape.

One of the leaders in this blurring of boundaries between words and images was Marcel Duchamp, who said that "words are not *merely* a means of communication"[34] but as much a symbol for the artist as the vase in a still life. In his own way, Ohr sensed this symbiosis between language and his pots. In a poster on his pottery, he declaims, "Deeds are Fruits, Words are Leaves" (Figure 22), suggesting a causal relationship between the two.

Figure 109
Ohr proclamation, published as an advertisement in the *Philistine: A Periodical of Protest* 14, no. 1 (Dec. 1901), facing p. 1.

REV. GEORGE E. OHR begs to introduce himself to the Philistines as

Potter to the Push

also

Originator of the Bug-House Renaissance in Life, Letters and Art. Mr. Ohr, like Setebos, makes things out of Mud—and never duplicates. Correspondence solicited. Address,

BILOXI, MISS.

☞ P. S. Mr. Ohr wishes to explain that the prefix Rev. to his name does not signify that he is a preacher. It only means that he is worthy of Reverence, because he does his work as well as he can, and Minds his own Business.

Figure 110
Ohr leaning against the west wall of
the pottery.

created posters, and printed handbills. He even
played with what might be defined today as a
structuralist investigation of words, giving each
of his children a first name that was also his or
her three initials: Oto, Clo, Ojo, Flo, Geo, Leo,
and Lio.

Ohr also realized that the artist could trans-
figure language much as he could shape clay.
As Duchamp maintained, "because language is
an imperfect form of communication . . . to
make yourself understood you have to create
words your neighbor can understand."[35] Ohr
went about creating a language that was as
inventive, energetic, and rhythmically complex
as any of his pots.

In particular Ohr enjoyed the pun. His puns
were not the elegant theoretical speculations
about grammatical relations and phonetic
structures that Duchamp was so adroit at creating. Ohr's language and wit were considerably
more down-home. He worked in a pottery surrounded by signs that read MY NAME IS MUD, GET

Words surrounded Ohr's art. He nailed slogans
to his wall and performed at fairs under ban-
ners declaring him to be the "Greatest Art
Potter in the World." He wrote manifestos,
published letters, scribbled verses on his pots,

Figure 111
Ohr's *Nine O'Clock in the Evening* and
Three O'Clock in the Morning, c.
1900. National Museum of History
and Technology, The Smithsonian
Institution, Washington, D.C.

ON 2 MY EARTHEN-WAR, POT-OHR-E, and others. Then there were his brothel tokens with their mix of words, phonetic sounds, and images.

Ohr sometimes titled works to alter their meaning or context. One of the best examples of this is a pair of top hats in the collection of the Smithsonian Institution. The first hat, entitled *Nine O'Clock in the Evening,* is pristine and perfect, while the second, *Three O'Clock in the Morning,* is torn and collapsed. This use of lowbrow, verbal/visual humor has a particular place in the ceramics and sculpture of the Funk movement, particularly in the work of Arneson, whose *Call Girl* (1967) shows a telephone with pendulous breasts.

Ohr's zaniest wordplay comes in his letters. What they lack in literary finesse, they more than make up for in spunk and spark. Ohr's writing has an identifiable affinity with the distinctive cadences of Robert Browning's poetry, as the New York newspaper writer so perceptively pointed out. Almost undecipherable at first, the sense—and structure—of his sputtering, popping stream of consciousness emerges with several readings.

One of Ohr's most interesting "documents" is a paragraph inscribed, appropriately, on the base of a pot. (The main text of the letter appears in Appendix B.) It is addressed to the Smithsonian, the institution he had hoped would purchase his entire collection of work.

To the Smithsonian
Washington
As Kind words, and deeds never Die
Sutch words and deeds are
"Fire-Waters" Acid
and "Time proof." When recorded on Mother
Earth-or clay-This is an empty Jar. Just
like the world.... Deed and thoughts live But the
instigators are shadows—fade and disappear
when the sun goes DOWN
Mary had a little lamb "Pot-Ohr-E-George"
has (HAD) *a little* Pottery *"Now" where*
is the Boy that stood in the Burning
Deck. "This Pot is here," and
I am the Potter Who was
G.E. Ohr

Ohr used language in many ways. First, language fed his involvement in symbolism. Second, it helped him create a theatrical fantasy world wherein he *was* the greatest art potter. As Jervis so unkindly reminds us, "He said so and he ought to know."[36] This self-aggrandizement created an aura of success for Ohr when, in fact, no such recognition existed. Perhaps it was one of his devices for keeping his faith.

While few would claim an exalted station for Ohr's writing, it was an important element in his art making and his creative process, which he incorporated into almost every aspect of his work and life. In an innocent way Ohr had grasped a highly sophisticated means of symbolization that later vitalized the fine arts in the twentieth century. Ohr's words enlarge upon his aesthetic discourse and remain, outside the pots themselves, the most revealing and exciting insight into his inventive spirit and sustaining energy.

Figure 112
Large umbrella stand, 1900. The vase carries a lengthy incised letter to the Smithsonian Institution from Ohr, reproduced in full in Appendix B. National Museum of History and Technology, The Smithsonian Institution, Washington, D.C.

Ohr the Clown

Truly wise men have no other mission than to make us laugh with their thoughts and make us think with their buffoonery.

Octavio Paz, The Castle of Purity

Ohr first exploited his remarkable theatrical persona as a means of huckstering and attracting attention to his work. Later the role became more complex, and it is difficult to determine who was manipulating the strings when Ohr played the fool or indulged in what he termed "stunting." Was Ohr simply playing at being the fool or was Octavio Paz's "truly wise" man subconsciously pulling the strings?

In a letter to Robert Blasberg, Cox reported a conversation he had with Ohr towards the end of his life. It is a touching commentary on Ohr's role as the clown: "He sat on the bed blinking his black eyes at me. Finally he said, 'You think I am crazy don't you?' I replied that Meyer had told me about him and that I did not think he was crazy. (I Still don't.) With that George stopped his act and remarked, 'I found out a long time ago that it paid me to act that way.'"[37]

Some saw beyond Ohr's personality. Hutson, remarking upon Ohr's flair for the extravagant, likened him to Whistler, another notorious self-promoter, but noted that Ohr could not be accused of the humbuggery of Hubbard for "Mr. Ohr is nothing if not an original."[38]

For many, however, Ohr's stunting became his most valued talent, and his promotional activities ended up achieving the opposite of their intent, blinding his audience to his sincerity and sensitivity with his noisy, brash fairground brouhaha. In 1899 a writer for the *China, Glass and Pottery Review* remarked that Ohr, "a naturally bright, even brilliant man, has been led to the belief that the way for him to attain publicity is through the channel of preposterous advertising [which does] him more harm than good." The writer felt that his antics brought on ridicule and mistrust and that he would be better off coming to New York and placing his affairs "under the guidance of some reputable house where his affairs could be conducted in a dignified spirit."[39]

Figures 113–14
In these photographs, taken as a set in the latter 1890s, Ohr is actually standing on the floor, while objects such as the hat and the bucket are attached to the ceiling.

Whats the matter Eh! well!
People there is plenty the matter. Soposen a pretty " a beautiful"--a raving handsome and
sweet darling steen years of
lovlyness--were 2 tell U--right
at Y-R mustach--that U was the
sweetest man on Earth and was
going 2 love U 4 Y-R life--heart
& soul; wouldent you shout very
loud, and nervously the word--
W H A T. Dats nuff matter,

Figure 115
Ohr uses his eighteen-inch moustache as a prop in this bizarre but amusing portrait, c. 1900; from the Ohr family album.

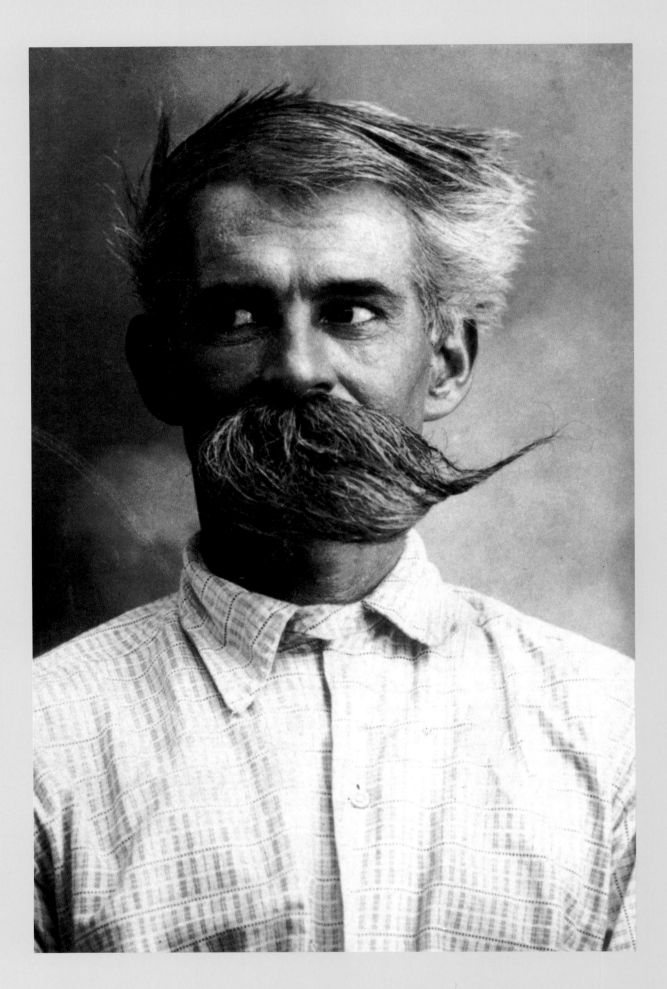

Figure 116
Photo from the Ohr family album, c.
1900.

Ohr's manner *did* serve to alienate him from the very audience he sought to attract. The Arts and Crafts Movement was a bourgeois club, and those among its ranks who did not come from the middle classes soon affected the manner of that class. Ohr's rusticity clashed with their self-image of genteel bohemianism. The criticism of Frederick Hurten Rhead that Ohr was "entirely without art training and altogether lacking in taste" summed up the disdain of the movement for vulgar or eccentric behavior.[40]

The movement was more concerned with formal skills and conventional beauty than with originality. Indeed within the art pottery movement, where copying the popular designs from Europe was the order of the day, Ohr's fresh and unique vision must have caused some discomfort and guilt. Furthermore, to the movement's East Coast leadership, Ohr was not simply a loudmouthed bumpkin. He was, even worse, a *Southern* bumpkin.

What, then, was Ohr's purpose in his self-promotion? He did not seek commercial success. As almost every interviewer pointed out, Ohr had a "splendid disdain" for money. He asked for his pots' weight in gold as a symbolic gesture of giving his work the highest material value that his culture could assign it. And loath to sell his clay babies, Ohr knew well that no one would be prepared to pay his price. In 1900 he was asking twenty-five dollars for a vase. Even his contemporary Adelaide Robineau, whose work in porcelain was very precious, accessible, and desirable, found it difficult fifteen years later to obtain a mere thirty-five dollars for her complex, carved vessels.[41]

It is interesting that the only potter Ohr appeared to admire was Bernard Palissy (1510–90), who suffered the same problem in his lifetime, becoming known for his antics rather than his art. Ohr drew considerable comfort from his identification with Palissy, calling himself the "second Palissy." A French mannerist who acquired a considerable reputation for his bizarre behavior, Palissy was a deeply religious man and an inventive artist. Even though he was appointed "Inventor of the King's Rustic Pottery" in 1652, his work was largely unappreciated in his day. He was an intellectual and a

Figure 117
An example of Ohr's love of photographic stunting: the Ohr "twins" toast each other with a tankard of beer, around 1905.

more rational philosopher than Ohr, but his writings display the same feverish energy, the same disdain for the establishment, and a distrust of the ordinary. Above all one senses the same obsessive search for the new, a mission he followed regardless of its cost or consequences.

A writer for the *Clay Worker* saw the connection between the two mavericks. "With his own hands [Ohr] fired the kiln, using wood for the purpose; one can easily imagine that, like Palissy, if his wood and money ran short at a critical moment in the firing, he might be capable of breaking up his furniture to keep up the fire."[42] While it is undisputed that Ohr drew inspiration from Palissy's travails, it is unclear whether the mannerist's pottery had an influence on his own. It is possible that Ohr's incongruous reptiles have their root in Palissy's own fondness for snakes and lizards in his relief decoration. The palette of the two artists is similar, particularly if one examines the undersides of a Palissy vessel.[43]

Ohr's knowledge of Palissy derived from a revival of interest in the artist in the mid-nineteenth century. At that time many books were published on Palissy, including Cecilia L. Brightwell's *Palissy the Potter; Or the Huguenot, Artist and Martyr. A True Account* (1858)

Figure 118
George E. Ohr standing in his pottery shortly after the fire, probably around 1896, with his wife, Josephine, and the kids, Lio, Leo, Clo (in the back), baby Oto, and the family cat. Smoke pours from the small kiln salvaged from the fire in 1894.

and Robert Morley's *Palissy the Potter* (1853). In addition numerous apocryphal articles appeared throughout the nineteenth century in the popular press and in such ceramic trade publications as the *Clay Worker*.

While Ohr certainly saw engraved illustrations of Palissy's pots, he could not easily have observed the work itself. There is no record of any exhibitions of work by Palissy or the nineteenth-century school of *Palissystes* in the New Or-

leans area during Ohr's lifetime.[44] Until there is conclusive proof, one must simply assume that Palissy's primary role in Ohr's life was that of a companion, an alter ego, and a fellow clown who lessened the sense of isolation that Ohr endured for most of his career as an art potter.

Ohr's stunting did not stop with his self-promotion, but included this potter's love of bizarre photography. As with so many of his interests, this activity might at first appear somewhat banal. Trick photography was a populist interest, a funfair divertissement. Some pictures, such as the portraits of the Ohr twins toasting each other, are the standard stock-in-trade of such photography, and despite their considerable charm, are in no way remarkable.

But when one begins to assemble a group of Ohr's bizarre photographs, one can again sense the obsession and transfiguration that converts the commonplace to the extraordinary in Ohr's art. Using his moustache as a prop he commissioned a series of highly dramatic portraits in which one senses the "pre-Surrealism Surrealist" (complete with his pre-Dali moustache) to whom Coplans referred earlier (Figures 115, 116). These photographs extend beyond casual stunting to take on the presence of highly exploratory and expressive self-portraits.

The photograph that is arguably the most significant of the group shows Ohr after the fire that destroyed his pottery. With his family arranged in pots (even a stuffed doll has been set inside a large clay eggshell), his "babies" have been returned to the womb. The photograph, whether intentionally or not, symbolizes Ohr's rebirth or resurrection, for after the fire his work developed a smoldering radicalism that, in the next decade, produced nearly all of Ohr's true art pots.

While Ohr's photographs are not important in themselves, they raise the same questions that critic John Perreault posed of Ohr's writing: "Is this madness, poetry or wisdom? Can we separate the charlatan/trickster aspects of Ohr's career from his vision and achievement?"[45] The answer is that the two aspects of the work probably cannot be separated. Nor do they need to be. The elements of Ohr's eccentric life and career—his theomorphism, eroticism, wordplay, pots, stunts, surrealist photographs, his three-foot-long moustache and Barnum routines—all were part of a dense laminate that made up one of the most fascinating and innovative individuals of the turn of the century.

Ohr probably did not mean to play the clown all his life. At first he exploited his naturally ebullient personality to obtain publicity. Later he used it to shield himself from the indiffer-

Figure 119
George in the backyard of the pottery sometime around 1900.

ence to, or dislike of, his art. Eventually it became as much a part of his art as his pots and he could no more adjust his personality to conventional behavior than he could trim his pots into conventional shapes. He was considered curious (or "queer," to use the vernacular of his day) even for an artist. But had Ohr been found slumming with Dada artists at the Cabaret Voltaire in the 1910s or performing at the soirees of the Surrealists in the 1920s, his behavior would have been, if not commonplace, at least identifiably part of the new theatricality that had in-

Figure 120
Betty Woodman, *Aegean Pillow Pitcher*,
1986. Private collection, New York.

Figure 121
Rudolf Staffel, *Untitled Vase*, 1975.
Daniel Jacobs, New York.

vaded the visual arts. As Paz writes, "all the limited number of men who have dared to be free have chosen (or been chosen) to play the clown."[46]

The Reappraisal

George Ohr is a great artist.

John Perreault, Village Voice, *1985*

Ohr's reappraisal began with the arrival of his ouevre in the marketplace in 1972[47] and was greeted with some excitement by the "product-hungry" art pottery collectors. Curators and historians of the decorative arts and the Arts and Crafts Movement, however, were still ill at ease with Ohr's lack of middle-class credentials, with his "Ohr ful" punning, his history of coarse promotional activities, and his explicit sexual obsessions.

Some curators and historians preferred to categorize Ohr as a folk artist, thus keeping the decorative arts neighborhood "pure," in a formalist sense, and neutralizing Ohr's iconoclasm. But Ohr does not fit the role of folk artist very well. Undoubtedly folk pottery strongly influenced his early work. And in his social standing Ohr fits more conveniently into the shacks of the folk potter than the elegant salons of the Arts and Crafts Movement. But in the final analysis, Ohr lacks the true isolation and fragile naivete of the folk potter. He was, in fact, very well informed about his field and far too sophisticated in his knowledge and intent to find a place in the more innocent world of folk art. There was an attempt made in the 1980s to exhibit Ohr at the Museum of American Folk Art in New York City, but it was dropped in the face of vigorous opposition from Ohr collectors who saw this as inappropriate.

Curatorial attitudes have changed, however, and Ohr's pieces have recently been acquired by many museums, including the Metropolitan Museum of Art, the Museum of Modern Art, the Cooper-Hewitt Museum, and the Brooklyn Museum in New York City, the Los Angeles County Museum, and the Victoria and Albert Museum in London.

From the outset, however, Ohr began to attract another kind of audience—the one he had sought to engage in his own lifetime—the so-called high arts of the contemporary art world of New York City. First critic John Coplans and dealer Irving Blum began to collect Ohr's work. Soon the word spread and Ohr began to attract a distinguished group of fine-arts devotees from Andy Warhol to Jasper Johns. What eased the passage of Ohr's work into these circles was the revolution that had been taking place in the mid-fifties in American ceramics. Led first by Voulkos, and later by Arneson, American ceramists had completely overturned the medium's adherence to passive, tasteful aesthetics. Pots were torn, punctured, broken, and reassembled. Tasteful urns were replaced by Funk toilets with fecal contents. Surface "decoration" was replaced with vigorous painting. Not only did the character of American ceramics change, but the movement had a dramatic impact on ceramics worldwide, establishing America as its avant-garde center.

By the time Ohr's work became generally known to the ceramics world in the late seventies and early eighties, there was already something of an Ohr "school" of clay handling in existence. Apart from the work of Arneson and Voulkos, others were now pushing the vessel to an expressionistic edge. Rudolf Staffel created tight, distorted forms in a dry porcelain clay influenced by the push-pull abstractions of his painting teacher Hans Hofmann. Betty Woodman was applying glazes and handles with the same freedom and theatrical invention as Ohr. These artists arrived at their material "solutions" between the 1950s and 1970s without any knowledge of Ohr. Ohr's reappearance, with such a daringly expressive vocabulary of clay handling, endorsed and confirmed the vision of those artists already working with a similar syntax. Conversely, the fact that so many contemporary ceramists had come to the same solutions as Ohr bore out his prophecy.

The event that brought Ohr to the attention of the art world at large was an exhibition in 1984 of paintings by Jasper Johns, at the Castelli Gallery in New York. It was Johns's first major show in some years and it attracted a great deal of attention. His paintings dealt with many fragments from his past and also with a new

obsession: the pots of George Ohr. These vessels were central images in Johns's work, painted with what *New York Times* reviewer John Russell termed "a touching fidelity."[48] This was a tender, moving homage from one American master to another.

In 1985 a loan exhibition exploring Ohr's acceptance within the fine arts was organized at

Figure 122
Jasper Johns, *Ventriloquist*, 1983.
Museum of Fine Arts, Houston.

Figure 123
Portrait of George Edgar Ohr, c. 1900.

the Garth Clark Gallery in New York. This was Ohr's first individual exhibition in New York City, and his works were borrowed from several art world collections, including those of Johns, Blum, and Cowles. Reviewing it in the *Voice*, John Perreault confirmed Ohr's belief in his own genius while commenting that the exhibition was merely a tease: "But what a tease; look at each vessel as a sculpture occupying space and time; look at each vessel as a painting. Then see all these things simultaneously, along with the wit—handles stuck here and there, the elegant accidents, the crush and twist. George Ohr is a great artist."[49]

Ohr is now prominently posited within the world of art. He will have to endure further scrutiny, but he is no longer viewed as a screwball, nor as a romantic preserver of handicraft ideals. Ohr has proved that the humble pot can make a contribution to the avant-garde in twentieth-century art. He set a standard for expressionism in clay that remains intimidating and provocative. Moreover, Ohr has finally escaped the classicist snobbery of the Arts and Crafts Movement and has taken on the *public* mantle of an artist. He has at last achieved his zeitgeist, but like most prophets, his acceptance and understanding has arrived in an era far distant from his own.

Plate 90   Handled vase, c. 1895–1900. Height: 9⅞ inches. Private collection, New York.

Plate 91   Handled vase, c. 1895–1900. Height: 9¼ inches. Private collection, New York.

Plate 92
Vase, c. 1895–1900.
Height: 9 inches. Private collection,
New York City.

Plate 93
Vase, c. 1895–1900.
Height: 7½ inches. Private collection,
Montague, New Jersey.

Plate 94
Vase, c. 1895–1900.
Height: 4¾ inches. Private collection,
Montague, New Jersey.

Plate 95
Vase, c. 1895–1900.
Height: 6¾ inches. Private collection,
New York.

148

Plate 96   Vase, c. 1895–1900. Height: 7¼ inches. Private collection, New York City.

Plate 97   Handled vase, c. 1895–1900. Height: 6¾ inches. Private collection, New York.

Plate 98   Handled vase, c. 1895–1900. Height: 8 inches. Private collection, New York City.

Plate 99
Vase, c. 1895–1900.
Height: 3⅝ inches. Private collection,
New York.

Plate 100
Vase, c. 1898–1907.
Height: 4½ inches. Private collection,
Montague, New Jersey.

Plate 101
Vase, c. 1895–1900.
Height: 3⅞ inches. Private collection,
New York.

Plate 102   Handled vase, c. 1895–1900. Height: 8 inches. Private collection, New York City.

Plate 103   Tall vase, c. 1895–1900. Height: 13½ inches. Jean and Martin Mensch, New York City.

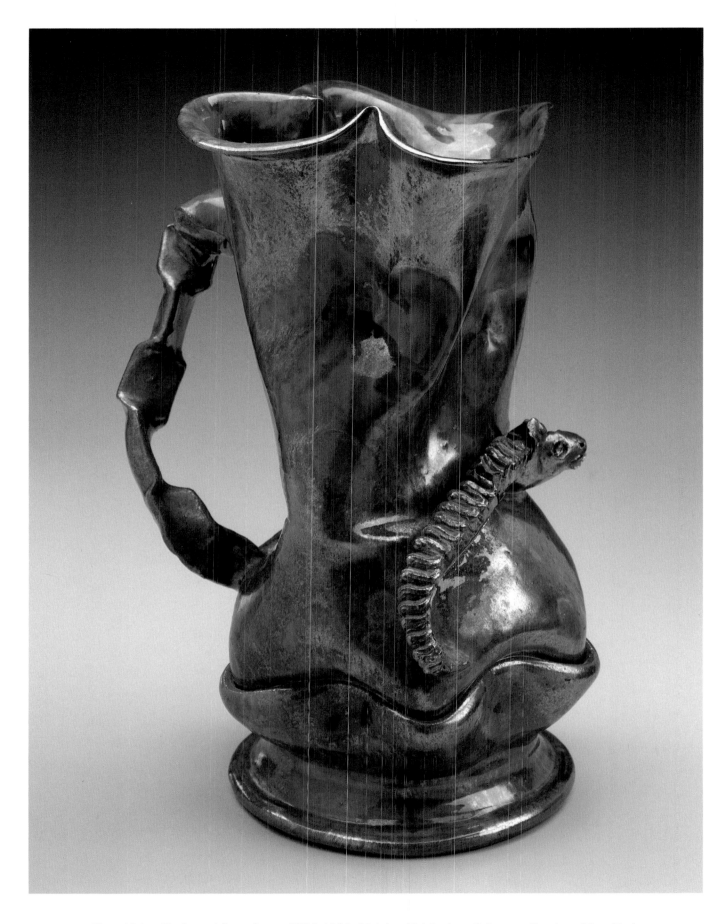

Plate 104   Pitcher with snake, c. 1895–1900. Height: 7½ inches. Private collection, New York.

Plate 105
Small vase, c. 1898.
Height: 3¼ inches. Charles Cowles, New York City.

Plate 106
Small vase, c. 1890–95.
Height: 4 inches. Private collection, New York City.

Plate 107
Small handled cup, c. 1898–1907.
Height: 3¾ inches. Private collection, New York.

Plate 108   Small bowl, c. 1895–1900. Height: 4 inches. Private collection, New York.

Plate 109   Footed vase, c. 1895–1900. Height: 7½ inches. Private collection, New York City.

Plate 110
Vase, c. 1895–1900.
Height: 7½ inches. Private collection, New York City.

Plate 111
Vase, c. 1898.
Height: 6½ inches. Patti Lel Smith-Zanone,
Memphis, Tennessee.

Plate 112
Vase, c. 1895–1900.
Height: 5 inches. Herman and Janice Zuckerman,
New York City.

Plate 113
Vase, c. 1898.
Height: 6¼ inches. Irving Blum, New York City.

Plate 114
Cup, c. 1898–1907.
Height: 4½ inches. Private collection,
Montague, New Jersey.

Plate 115
Vase, c. 1900.
Height: 6¾ inches. Mr. and Mrs Dennis Berard,
Fitzwilliam, New Hampshire.

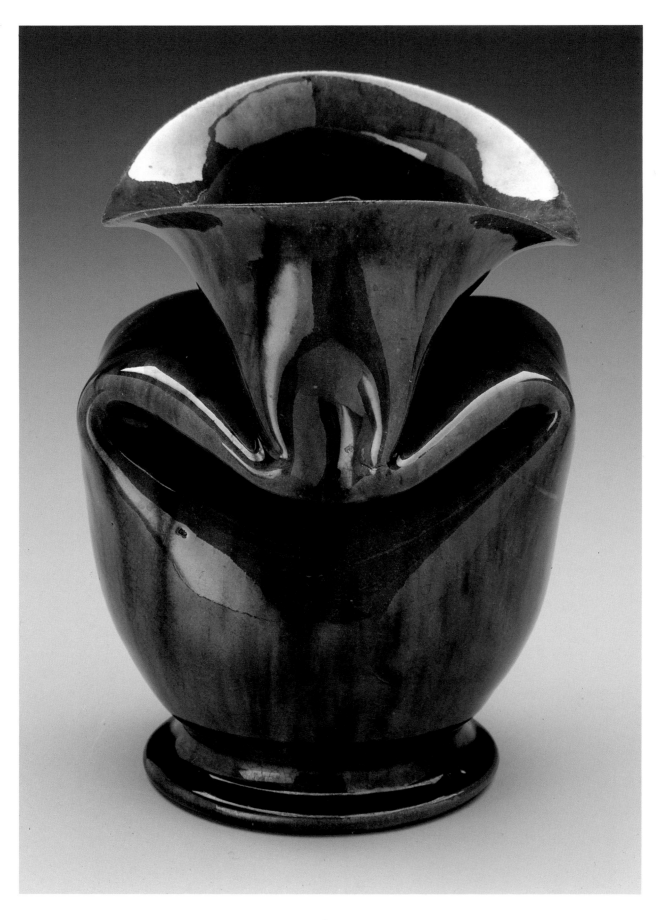

Plate 116   Vase, c. 1895–1900. Height: 6 inches. Private collection, New York City.

Plate 117
Vase, c. 1895–1900.
Height: 5 inches. Arthur F. and Esther Goldberg,
Closter, New Jersey.

Plate 118
Vase, c. 1895–1900.
Height: 7½ inches. Private collection, New York City.

Plate 119   Teapot, c. 1895–1900. Height: 10 inches. Private collection, New York.

Plate 120   Teapot, c. 1895–1900. Height: 7¾ inches. Private collection, New York City.

Plate 121
Vase, c. 1895–1900.
Height: 3¾ inches. Private collection, New York.

Plate 122
Vase, c. 1898–1907.
Height: 5½ inches. Private collection, New York.

Plate 123   Teapot, c. 1895–1900. Height: 3½ inches. Private collection, New York.

Plate 124   Teapot with snakes, front and back views, c. 1895–1900. Height: 4⅝ inches. Private collection, New York City.

Plate 125 Cadogan teapot with double spouts, c. 1895–1900. Height: 8 inches. Robert Tannen, New Orleans.

Plate 126
Vase, c. 1898.
Height: 6 inches. Charles Cowles,
New York City.

Plate 127
Vase, c. 1895–1900.
Height: 6⅜ inches. Private collection,
New York.

Plate 128   Cadogan teapot, c. 1898–1907. Height: 5½ inches. Private collection, New York.

Plate 129   Teapot, c. 1895–1900. Height: 6⅜ inches. Private collection, New York.

Plate 130   Teapot, c. 1902. Height: 6½ inches. Jederman N.A., Princeton, New Jersey.

Plate 131
Pitcher, c. 1900.
Height: 8½ inches. Charles Cowles, New York City.

Plate 132
Pitcher, c. 1895–1900.
Height: 9 inches. Private collection, New York City.

Plate 133 Three-handled mug, c. 1900. Height: 8 inches. Jasper Johns, New York City.

My grandfather, John Geo. Ohr, with his wife and one son, came to America from Alsace in 1850. That son was the only one, and a blacksmith complete and outright. He was born in 1819. His parents died in New Orleans in 1852. My mother, Johanna Wiedman, came from Wurtenberg. Those two met in New Orleans in 1853, and after a rag-chewing time of a few hours the Alsace blacksmith seemed to be good looking, etc., enough for Johanna, so they locked horns and pulled their local and freight to and for Biloxi, Miss., U.S.A., on a steamboat or schooner—as I wasn't there you can guess which (all guesses will be considered correct by me). Suffice to say that 1819 Ohr shod the first horse in this second oldest town in the U.S.

I came on the second schooner, and knocked the nose out of joint of the first one, and kept it so, as the other three storks that came in town were nothing to brag about, and that completed the programme (3 hens, 1 rooster and a duck—I'm that duck. I don't know how it happened, but it did, and was no fault of mine).

The cuckoo is a swindle, and had I been on the cuckoo order my name would have been Dennis McGintymud. As it is—and was—I had a big load to haul, and survived many catastrophes besides getting all the lickings of the family, as everything that was ever done wrong or happened around 3 corners, or if it did not rain, or rained too much, or the clock wouldn't tick, or someone's horse ran away, and 1,000 other things went democrat, I caught L for it. Oh! I tell you! I've had some fun in my 44 years, running away from danger and getting caught with open arms every time. Suppose 5 hen eggs were put under a brood and somebody somewhere made a mistake and got a duck egg in the job lot, that duck is going to be in some very hot aqua and evaporated, liquified air.

Well, I stormed the weather until I remember having cold bare feet about 18 times and the water was getting so almighty darned hot that I concluded not to be in it all the time, and changed boarding places 80 miles away (New Orleans, La.).

I found a free hash house and did free work as compensation for 3 months, and soap thrown in to do my own washing. You read about rag-time doings on top of your New York sky scrapers! Well, to have a genuine rag-pushing time you ought to have seen me while at that ship-chandler's store as chief cook for all hands. As I had to

work as soon as I was able to walk—there was none of any kind that I could be made to run or shrink from—I held the warehouse job at the ship's grocer's for 2 years. But that old boss sponge believed in working the hide and hair from a cheap young mule. My 3d year's salary was raised to 15 dollars per month and no charge for soap. As I did a man's work, and as $1.50 per day (15 hours) was a man's wages, I excused myself to the old badger.

Going home to Biloxi again, I did more different work than one can count on finger tips.

Previous to the above I went to German school in New Orleans one winter; the following winter an apprentice in a file cutter's shop; another winter in a tinker's shop; then came the ship store.

The next thing was a letter from J. F. Meyer (now the Sophy Newcome potter) who knew me before I did him (the reason for that, he is about 10 years older). That letter done it—$10 a month and a chance to swipe a trade!

As usual, I pulled up stakes, stole a freight train at 11:65, and p.d.q. went under the night and over terra firma—and I don't think up to this day that Supt. Marshall, of the L. & N R. R. ever suspected or thought of searching me for his freight train.

After working at about 14 professions and that many businesses also, and remembering what the old lady private school teacher told me once—to always fill a want—when I found the potter's wheel I felt it all over like a wild duck in water. After knowing how to boss a little piece of clay into a gallon jug I pulled out of New Orleans and took a zigzag trip for 2 years, and got as far as Dubuque, Milwaukee, Albany, down the Hudson, and zigzag back home. I sized up every potter and pottery in 16 States, and never missed a show window, illustration or literary dab on ceramics since that time, 1881.

I managed to economize, and in 2 years more, working in New Orleans, I saved up a huge wad of the green stuff which took me 3 hours to count (taking lots of time). I spent more than 3 hours wondering how I was going to have a full-equipped pottery for 2680 cents. Well, I done it (and done it twice—burned out 2d time). As I was an ex-blacksmith, I made the iron work, the clay mill and potter's wheel. My capital was all put into brick for the kiln. I put up the mill and made clay mortar, and like the mud wasp made my kiln with lime, then with grit and credit; got hold of some pine trees (saw logs), had 'em

sawed up on shares, and rafted the lumber about 18 miles down a river. Hauled the lumber all myself and built the first shop all alone. As I had a home and was not accustomed to pay board, washing, or anything of the sort, I was a dead beat all right. The old man kicked like a circus mule as to the amount and size of the stuff I was swiping, but mamma said: "Let the boy go on, and watch him."

I had to do lots of work, and hard and heavy. But all is light and easy when the will and love of it is there, and when one gets really enthusiastic they will forget to get hungry. It happened only once with me. I forgot or had no time to go to dinner, and when supper time came I thought and thought, and wondered if I was a Republican carpet-bagger or a middle of the road Democrat, or vice versa. But in the morning I solved it—I was a going potter. Eat or no eat, money or no money, sweetheart dead or not born, it was all the same to me.

The first year I got enough dimes to cover my frame, but not to fill it up. That was in 1883, the year of the New Orleans Cotton Centennial Exposition. I had over 600 pieces, no two alike, there. It cost me my total year's savings to show up, and as I got the wrong man to attend to the taking away of my ware, stand and fixings, it turned out to be nobody's business and everybody's pottery.

Well, I've made some more, and you can't keep a live squirrel on the ground; and the New Orleans Exposition is out of sight, and so are those mud fixings.

Everybody knows it's bad to push a good thing too far, and a darned sight worse to shove a worse thing farther; so right here I'll drive a stake down and put a ground wire.

For further or more information concerning my get-up and get-there, careering, maneuvering and canoeing, write to the paddler of Bilox's mud flat, whose name is   Geo. E. Ohr

Printed in *Crockery and Glass Journal* 54 (12 December 1901). Photo courtesy Science and Technology Research Center, The New York Public Library, Astor, Lenox and Tilden Foundations.

Appendix A

Some Facts in the History of a Unique Personality.

Autobiography of Geo. E. Ohr, the Biloxi Potter.

Appendix B

Text inscribed on
umbrella stand, c. 1900.

The following text was inscribed by Ohr on a large umbrella stand that he created for the Smithsonian Institution but never delivered (although it is now in their collection; catalog #78.4, National Museum of History and Technology).

Text around stand below rim:

The Somebody (that used to be) that 'made this Pot' Was born at Biloxi, Miss—July 12, 1857 (on Sunday 10.AM sharp) and is and was G. E. Ohr"—

Incised in vertical lines on sides of the stand is the following text:

Dear George

Your letter of recent date has been received. In the long interval that has elapsed since I and you have seen each other, at no time have I forgotten the struggling genius hidden in small Biloxi, like a precious stone in mothe earth-perhaps. never found- and as the years roll on and the final summons come, *Art* and *Genius* will foreever sleep,—the world no wiser,—except' the remaining few. whos memory may still recall the *demented Potter* in his silent grave.

Forgive me brother, if too pointed. I am simply Illustrating the Past, present and Future! How often in the two years that I lived and struggled in your beautiful littly city. I could have crushed. if I dared. those thos who know in their hearts that the man, whom they flung that vile, selfish and unjust epithet at: *Demented Potter.* had more brains in one Ioto of his body than 9/10 of Biloxies whole population put together!.

Peculiar Biloxi. and its Peculiar people, I shall allway remember the beautiful summer night that sentence was express. Corn Pass Christian and Lamuse Sts. by one whom I still believe had a right to know and how often after that: while struggling in the burning heat those summer days in my little broom factory toiling. from early morn. untill late at night, and which none can deny, to accomplish for those whom I dearly loved. simple a humble home and our daily food. had that same sentence gone home to me: You state. I have not ben missed: fear. not friend. I have not thought otherwise. but while nothing has benn lost, I still feel that nothing has has been gained in crushing and driving me away.

I once more live amongst those who consider me their equal and human like themselves. "My native Home." where men grasp my hand. whose wealth would equal any there. simply be cause I had the manhood to remark without affront to any one- That the City of Biloxi need a fearless paper like RE _ E _ (?) to strike without fear. or favor: I was condemned and crushed I was filling an order for 24 Dozen of Brooms at that time for a firm which was my only existance. immediately that order was cancelled. Had it been Russia at the time. no doubt my head would had paid the penalty.

If there is one thing I am proud of friend, and I challenge a contradiction. It's. "that. I left Biloxi-as I entered it" an honorable man and mark what I tell you. When man gets so that he believes he is beyond and above anothe being simply because fortune has smiled upon him," Providence the Almighty Ruler sais halt, you have gone far enoughf and when he strikes he humbles them again!

In justic to the few, who looked to the welfare of Biloxis little Broom Factory and did their utmost to keep it there, I and my littele family. still and. always will remember. Forgive me. I have made this laborious enoughf. May God bless you and yours, and should there still be any that remember Biloxies humble Broom maker give them my best wishes, and remember them to me. Sincerely Henry Pfluger 1707 Tulane ave "n.o.: La"

Incised in script on interior of stand:

"that honest and brave feature editor (*J. Laila* (?) of the RE??? was murdered a few weeks later than date on outside letter He like this writing was put under and insider of Earth.

Incised in script on base:

Biloxi. Miss.
Dec - 18 - 1900
To the Smithsonian Washington
As Kind Words, and deeds never Die
Sutch words and deeds are "Fire-Waters" Acid and "Time proof."
When recorded on Mother Earth-or clay- This is an empty Jar. *Just* like the world, "solid in itself" yet. full on the surface! Deed and thoughts live But the instigators are shadows—fade and disapear when the Sun goes

DOWN Mary had a luttle lamb "Pot•Ohr•E•George has (HAD) a little *Pottery* "Now" where is the Boy that stood in the Burning Deck. "This Pot is here," and I am the Potter Who was G. E Ohr

The Times and Life of G. E. Ohr

1. Much of the chronology of Ohr's early life derives from his charming, though remarkably confusing and at times inaccurate, autobiographical account, "Some Facts in the History of a Unique Personality," *Crockery and Glass Journal* 54 (12 December 1901): p. 123 (see Appendix A). Accordingly, any reconstruction of the sequence of these events must by necessity be somewhat vague and a bit unreliable. Moreover, according to hearsay almost all of Ohr's personal documents (and there were trunks full) were wantonly destroyed by Leo, his oldest son. In his dotage the latter allegedly emptied the house of George's papers, abetted by a young lady friend, and fed a bonfire with them. As Oto Ohr tells it, when his father died "he left stacks of paper — stuff from the St. Louis Exposition, drawings, and everything. It was all carried to the backyard and set afire. I don't have any proof of this, but I understand this is what happened: all burned, nothing left. I did have a notebook, but I don't know where in the hell it is" (quoted from "Mississippi Trace," *Studio Potter* 10:2 (1981–82): p. 83). In his mid-80s, Leo confided that he hated his father because, as the oldest son, George made him do so much menial work around the pottery.

2. The time of his birth is provided by the inscription on an umbrella stand in the collection of the Smithsonian Institution (cat. # 78.4). Wiedman is the spelling of Ohr's mother's maiden name as it appears in his autobiography. An alternative, Widemann, exists in his father's will.

3. From an interview with his wife in the *New Orleans Times-Picayune*, 1 October 1922 (hereafter cited as *Times-Picayune*).

4. Suzanne Ormond and Mary E. Irvine, *Louisiana's Art Nouveau: The Crafts of Newcomb Style*, (Gretna, La.: Pelican Publishing, 1976), p. 12.

5. Meyer's obituary in the *Morning Tribune*, 17 March 1931, p. 2, cols. 3–5.

6. Meyer is listed in Soards' 1878 *New Orleans City Directory* as a potter; he is missing from the 1879 volume but appears again in the 1880 issue, as does George Ohr for the first time. Soards' was printed in February of each year, and given that it could have taken a few months to compile, Ohr's presence in the 1880 volume suggests that he was probably settled and gainfully employed in New Orleans during 1879.

7. Paul E. Cox, "Potteries of the Gulf Coast," *Ceramic Age* 3 (April 1935): p. 118.

8. Ohr, "A Unique Personality," p. 123.

9. He is listed in Soards' *Directory* of 1880 and 1881 as "Ohr George, potter."

10. There are no known unambiguously dated examples of the work from this earliest period. The hand-inscribed word *Biloxi* appears on what seem to be early specimens (ones that are certainly pre-1895) as well as on later ones. Similarly the mark consisting of a type-impressed GEO E. OHR centered over BILOXI and surrounded by a curved depression is also concluded to be among the first used. Another and possibly the earliest mark is the straight line GEO. E. OHR, BILOXI, MISS in small type. A little, unglazed jug covered with brown oil paint and decorated with an elaborate scene of water lilies carries a pencil date of 1879 and the straight-line impressed mark. The body seems unfused (unlike any other existing specimen of Ohr's pottery) and that lends some credibility to the early date. Ohr's own words on the subject suggest that he was using some sort of type mark as early as 1879: "A visitor asked me for my autograph and since then '1898' my creations are marked like a check. The previous 19 years mark is like any old newspaper type."

11. Ohr, "A Unique Personality," p. 123.

12. George was evidently in a rush to get into production and one might accordingly anticipate that this "pottery," which he put up "all alone" and fairly quickly, was of a very modest scale. In any event, no picture of any such structure, which is known to be from the early 1880s, exists. Moreover Ohr himself dates the erection of the earliest pottery building for which photos do survive as 1888 (Figure 4).

13. Ohr, "A Unique Personality," p. 123.

14. The thesis has been put forth that Ohr won an award at the Exposition. R. W. Blasberg, in *George E. Ohr and His Biloxi Art Pottery* (Port Jervis, N.Y.: J. W. Carpenter, 1973), p. 15, wrote, "We do know that he set up his booth at the New Orleans Cotton Exposition in the Eighties and won a medal." And in "Second Showing of the Pottery of George E. Ohr" in the program of the Gulf South Ceramic Show, October 1967. p. 9, Dolores Smith (who was a friend of the Ohr family, a source for Blasberg, and one of Ohr's first modern supporters) wrote, "George Ohr exhibiting as early as 1885 . . .won top honors at the New Orleans Cotton Exposition."

Nonetheless, no evidence from the period to that effect is known to be extant. Moreover it seems unlikely that Ohr would have neglected to remind us of such an early crucial award in either his autobiography (Ohr, "A Unique Personality") or previous interviews.

15. Mr. Howard was a wealthy Southern philanthropist who gave away enough money to have streets in both New Orleans and Biloxi renamed after him.

16. It is conceivable that this was only a part-time job for Meyer. In any case, he continues to be listed in the city directory (1887 to 1889) as a dealer of boots and shoes.

17. Her maiden name is entered as "Gerring" on the marriage license but that's probably an incorrect spelling.

18. *New Orleans Daily Picayune*, 11 December 1887, p. 4, col. 4.

19. Ralph J.. "In Sunny Mississippi," *Harper's New Monthly Magazine* 90 (May 1895): p. 819.

20. *New Orleans Daily Picayune*, 31 December 1893, p. 4, col. 5.

21. *Times-Picayune*.

22. Ralph Kovel and Terry Kovel, *The Kovels' Collectors Guide to American Art Pottery* (New York: Crown Publishers, 1974). p. 115.

23. Paul Evans, *Art Pottery of the United States* (Hanover, Pa.: Everybodys Press, 1974), p. 180.

24. *The Ladies, God Bless 'Em* (Cincinnati: Cincinnati Art Museum, 1976), pp. 25, 102. V. R. Cummins, ed., *Rookwood Pottery Potpourri*. (Silver Spring, Md.: C. R. Leonard and D. Coleman, 1980), p. 4.

25. A. F. Perry, "Decorative Pottery in Cincinnati," *Harper's New Monthly Magazine* 62 (May 1881): p. 837.

26. Josephine became pregnant with Leo E. sometime around December 1889, so George couldn't have been too far from home. Moreover dated examples of his work from 1891 carrying the Biloxi impression do exist (e.g., a bisque potato is marked *Mar, 26 1891*). Of course that in itself doesn't settle the question of Ohr's whereabouts.

27. According to (among others) Paul Cox, writing in 1935 ("Potteries of the Gulf Coast")."a cast of Ohr's arm forms part of the material for cast-drawing of Newcomb School of Art." This could have been an artifact left over from the days of the Ladies' Decorative Art League. In any event, it has long since vanished.

28. It seems likely that Ohr's travels of 1881 to 1882 may have taken him to the Kirkpatricks' pottery in Illinois. The brothers, Cornwall and Wallace, shipped stoneware from their factory at Anna to many major cities in the United States including New Orleans. It's possible that George could have first come in contact with their work there. In any event jugs draped with lifelike snakes, probably as a reflection of Wallace's views on temperance, were a favorite item there. In later years George produced jugs, often decorated by his assistant Portman, that are similar in some respects to certain of these early Anna pieces. [See Ellen P. Denker, *The Kirkpatricks' Pottery at Anna, Illinois* (Urbana-Champaign, Ill.: Krannert Art Museum, University of Illinois, 1986), p. 11, and compare that with R. and T. Kovel (*The Kovels' Collectors Guide to American Art Pottery*), color p. 5.] By contrast the reptiles on Ohr's artware are totally different and quite characteristic of his work. Another possible connection with the Kirkpatricks comes via their production of pig-shaped whiskey flasks. Though preceded by glass pig bottles, the Anna versions were quite popular in their own right. George made a stoneware pig flask glazed with Albany slip and dated "Mch. 25, 1882." The shape, glaze, clay body, and inscriptions are all similar to those of Anna and strongly suggest a connection. It is also possible that the double-vision trick photographs Ohr produced were a play on the obvious temperance message. There's usually some sort of alcoholic drink in the picture while George is split in two or stands on his head.

As for Ohr's own drinking habits we have the following account provided by Paul Cox, who knew George personally. In 1967 Cox, then 88 years old and quite ill, communicated his remembrances of the era in New Orleans (c. 1910) to R. Blasberg and that material has been made available by the latter's wife Faith. As Cox wrote: "I never had heard anything about George Ohr ever being drunk. Not that he could not have been a bit too overloaded as nobody of his time did without Dago Red with dinners. All I was ever told about his stunting was that he was touched a bit in the head. He had worked so long with all the folks I knew of the Newcomb College staff for me not to have been told he got a bit loaded with booze rather than what they did tell me which was that he was so much a clown in all he did that he was a nuisance." Cox letter, January 27, 1967.

29. Of course all of these decorative elements go back millennia, but it's important to note that they were in common use in America at the time. See, e.g., W. E. Wiltshire, *Folk Pottery of the Shenandoah Valley* (New York: E. P. Dutton, 1975).

30. A small, round-brimmed bisque hat inscribed *Aug 19th 1892* is the earliest dated example of this genre known to exist. One of the molds for the famous-house plaques is inscribed with the date 1892.

31. Ohr produced a variety of ceramic trinkets: tiny log cabins, card holders, bird whistles, musical instruments, ink wells, miniature shoes (remember Meyer's other occupation—he made clay shoes too), match safes, salts, and paperweights. Many potters of the period manufactured wares of this sort for the fair trade, including the Kirkpatricks. At the time, Lincoln log cabins were a ubiquitous symbol of America's youth— Ludwig Bauman and Company, Eighth Avenue New York (1898), offered little metal log cabin banks for twenty-nine cents.

32. At the very latest it is possible that this photo might date from around the summer of 1894, in which case the two children would be Leo and Clo.

33. W. A. King, "The Palissy of Biloxi," *Illustrated Buffalo Express,* 12 March 1899.

34. A small gray-green inkwell exists with the hand-incised inscription *Merry Xmas 1893 from Biloxi, Miss.*

35. *New Orleans Daily Picayune,* 13 October 1894.

36. Cox, "Potteries of the Gulf Coast," p. 110.

37. *New Orleans Daily Item,* 12 October 1894 (Friday evening), p. 8; *New Orleans Daily States,* 12 October 1894 (Friday), p. 2; *New Orleans Daily Picayune,* 13 October 1894 (Saturday), p. 1. George E. Ohr (like his father) carried no fire insurance and reported a property loss of three thousand dollars.

38. A vase survives marked *4–25–94* and signed *The Biloxi Potter.*

39. King, "The Palissy of Biloxi," p. 4.

40. There is a small, brown-glazed inkstand with a doubly ruffled neck carrying the inscription *First Piece on Small wheel Jan 12–95.* This is consistent with Ohr's claim to have rebuilt the pottery in 1894. He was also soon molding Mississippi mule-head and tiger-head inkwells—the plaster molds are dated 95 and 4–1–95, respectively.

41. Sometimes he threw pieces with walls so thin that the bases subsequently just dropped off. A stack of these vaseless bisque discs survives.

42. Cox, "Potteries of the Gulf Coast," p. 140. Cox thought highly of George as a technician but felt that "Ohr was a show off. And no designer. Arthur [Baggs] was the kind that would not agree with me about Ohr, for fear it would hurt feelings." Quoted from private correspondence with R. Blasberg, courtesy of Faith Blasberg. Baggs, like Cox, was one of the important ceramists of the American Arts and Crafts Movement.

43. A similar version of this poem appears set in the simulated type contained in a molded ceramic representation of a printer's type holder, which is marked *Jackson News 5–12–95.* See R. and T. Kovel, *The Kovels' Collectors Guide to American Art Pottery,* p. 147. Another just like it is marked *Biloxi Banner 5–15–95.* Ohr was quite pleased with this poem and he even impressed it into some of his ceramic price tags, which he wired onto many of his pieces.

44. "Concerning the Biloxi Potteries," *China, Glass and Pottery Review* 4 (April 1899): p. 47. This is unsigned but it looks like King's work.

45. Blasberg, *Ohr and His Biloxi Art Pottery,* p. 61.

46. Franklin M. Garrett, *Atlanta and Environs,* vol. 2 (New York: Lewis Historical Publishing Company, 1954), p. 311. Thanks are due to Nancy Wight of the Atlanta Historical Society.

47. Portman was born in May 1878 in Louisiana and died on June 13, 1917. He worked with Ohr as a potter from about 1895 to sometime around 1907. Harry is listed in the twelfth census of the United States (June 1900) as being in, and an employee of, the George Ohr (senior) household, having the occupation of potter. In the thirteenth census (April 1910), after George senior had passed away, Portman is listed as being the "adopted son" of George E. Ohr and having the occupation of lighthouse keeper on Round Island. There is a mold of a simple vase carrying Portman's conjoined JHP mark cut into the plaster along with *8–21. 1900.*

48. There are two placards in Figure 13 touting "Trilby photo in jug." Designed to be worn on a chain, these were miniature hollow ceramic bottles about 1¼ inches long with a glass-bead (Stanhope) lens at one end and open to admit light at the other. A tiny black-and-white positive transparency (roughly one or two millimeters on a side) was mounted to the back of the lens so that

when held close to the eye a magnified virtual image of the picture could clearly be seen. It's noteworthy that the Kirkpatricks at Anna had been making very much the same kind of device, with the transparencies prepared in Paris (see Denker, *Kirkpatricks' Pottery*, p. 13), since the early 1880s. The scheme was devised by Prudent René Patrice Dagron in France and patented in 1860. Little viewers of this sort set in jewelry and souvenirs were quite popular well into the present century. Ohr made a wonderful vase for his wife with two storks as handles and beneath a photo of it he attached the following message:

The Ohr-dity—Ohr-bout—the Ohr-Bove, Piece of Pot-Ohr. E—is—"that" a microscopical Photo" of myself and of she who loves my soul, can B seen by looking— R—taking a Birds Eye View in the Birds Eye-s,!...

It translates: the oddity about the above piece of pottery, etc.

49. Auction history was made in 1886 when a porcelain vase in the collection of Charles Morgan sold for eighteen thousand dollars. Hobbs, Brockunier and Company of Wheeling subsequently copied the piece in a colored glass that they called Peach Blow. An example of it is in the High Museum of Art in Atlanta, and George owned one too. Ohr waxed rancorous about counterfeits and how by comparison it was impossible to duplicate his work (see the little sign in Figure 18 and Figure 19). Ohr's little Peach Blown vase survives but it's not very exciting.

50. *Times-Picayune*. Jim Carpenter remembers seeing, sometime back in the 1960s, two medals that Ohr had won. It's possible that one of these was from Atlanta—the other was from St. Louis.

51. Mary Tracy Earle, *The Wonderful Wheel*, (New York: Century Company, 1896).

52. The mold for the Tarpon pitcher has the number 89 scratched into a smooth region on the bottom, but this is surrounded by a rough area that might possibly have obliterated some additional numbers. Still, 1889 is not an unreasonable date for its introduction based on its stylistic features and the marks on extant examples.

53. R. W. Blasberg, *The Unknown Ohr* (Milford, Pa.: Peaceable Press 1986), p. 28. There may exist some correlation between pitchers that were cast from already existing vessels and the presence of handles in the corresponding plaster molds. The early pitchers that are known to be Ohr's work were molded sans handles.

54. Austin Brereton, ed., *Gallery of Players* (New York: Illustrated American Publishing Company, 1894), p. 32.

55. "The Potter of Biloxi," *Crockery and Glass Journal* 70 (23 December 1909): p. 49.

56. See, for example, the catalogue for David Rago's *Collector's Spectrum* auction, November 1986, lot 25. Or R. and T. Kovel, *Kovels' Collectors Guide to American Art Pottery*, pp. 139 and 142. It was only after he had finished thirteen mugs that Ohr decided to number his production for the day. The rest are stamped *Previous to No. 14 Not Numbered* and hand inscribed with an appropriate number, the highest being around fifty-seven or so. He also made loving cups and it appears that he numbered them separately starting from one. Joseph Jefferson was a frequent visitor to the Rookwood Pottery whenever he played in Cincinnati and even tried decorating a few pieces of pottery when he was there. His toast appears on a jug decorated by A. M. Bookprinter (1886). So often did Jefferson pronounce that little bit of wisdom that by 1902 the Wharff-Eaton Company of Boston was selling a brass plaque inscribed with it and a sketch of old square-jawed J. J. dressed as Rip, mug in hand.

57. "The Potter of Biloxi," p. 49.

58. L. M. Bensel, "Biloxi Pottery," *Art Interchange* 46 (January 1901): p. 8.

59. Ibid.

60. King, "The Palissy of Biloxi," p. 4.

61. There is no extant documentation to verify that Ohr did in fact work at Newcomb or that he lived in New Orleans anywhere around that time— see Jessie Poesch, *Newcomb Pottery* (Exton, Pa.: Schiffer Publishing, 1984). The 1901 article by Bensel ("Biloxi Pottery"), which seems to be a firsthand account of a visit and interview with Ohr, remarks that "occasionally he goes to the Newcomb pottery, in New Orleans, to work." But Dr. Paul Cox (who knew Ohr) makes no mention of him being employed by Newcomb in his previously cited article, "Potteries of the Gulf Coast," or in "Notes and News, Newcomb Pottery Active in New Orleans," *American Ceramics Society Bulletin* 12 (1933): p. 140—though he does record Ohr's stay at the New Orleans Art Pottery. Cox came to Newcomb College in March 1910 to direct the technical operation of the pottery. His conversations with Meyer were the source of much of what he knew about the early days at Newcomb. "Meyer told me that Ohr learned the wheel from him. And Ohr

was such a nuisance with his nonsense that Newcomb Pottery could not use him for the work they had for a wheel potter. Meyer was a much steadier kind of intellect than Ohr." Cox letter March 4, 1967. Cox speaks about Ohr in these letters as though everyone at Newcomb (c. 1910) knew the Mad Potter and had a long, if not satisfying, working relationship with him.

62. Poesch, *Newcomb Pottery*, p. 94.

63. "Monsieur Jules Gabry's Wheel," *Brick* (May 1898): p. 220.

64. "A Biloxi Pottery," *Brick* (July 1897): p. 286. This account contains a brief history of Ohr's career and goes on to describe him as "a man of interesting conversation, with restless, flashing eyes."

65. Like most of his clay novelties, the concept of these little chamber pots was probably not original to Ohr. We do know the Kirkpatricks at Anna made mugs containing ceramic turd.

66. *Wallace Henley Dec. 4 1897* is inscribed on a small broken vase. A ruffled flowerpot bears the inscription *Marie K. Brooks/Ward W. Stringale, Jan. 20, 1898*. It can be inferred that some fraction of the vessels made for and inscribed by tourists were never picked up after being dried and fired days later. See David Rago's *Collector's Spectrum* auction catalogue, Nov. 1985, lot 228. R. and T. Kovel in *The Kovels' Collectors Guide to American Art Pottery*, picture a vase (p. 143) dated 1898. The fragment of the bottom of a pot reads: *Eng' Clay Ohr Biloxi 1899* written in script. And still another vase bears the inscription: *precious better-half Josie 7-4-1899*. A broken little pitcher is hand inscribed *S.C.G. Mch'3 1900* and then carries the strange mark *GEO* up at an angle; starting with that O it continues horizontally, *OHR Biloxi Miss*. A puzzle mug has the more traditional script signature (beginning with the O and doubling back) along with an inscribed *1900*. A bisque piece carries the hand-lettered inscription *April 1st 1901 a great day for fools and Smart Elicks*, (script signed) *GE Ohr, a fool in disguise that holds his own*.

67. With a few changes in capitalization and punctuation this is exactly stanza seventy-three in the fifth version (1889) of FitzGerald's translation of the *Rubáiyát*. The bottom of the piece bears the script signature of Augusta Semmes (a Mississippi resident), along with Ohr's signature and the type impression *G. E. OHR*, (centered over) *Biloxi, Miss,.* Interestingly, the bottom shows a date two days earlier, 3–30–99.

George also made a ceramic plaque depicting what seems to be the mouth of a kiln with flames and smoke curling around the words BILOXIES OHR MER KHAYAM.

68.   The author of "Concerning the Biloxi Potteries" (see note 44), quotes much of an article reputed to be from "a New York paper of the date of December 22, 1898." A search of New York newspapers, at least a dozen to date, has as yet not turned up that article. This includes the *New York Sun* mentioned in "Biloxi Pottery from an Artistic Standpoint," *China, Glass and Pottery Review* (June 1899): p. 20, which was also probably by W. A. King.

69.   King, "The Palissy of Biloxi," p. 4.

70.   Evans, *Art Pottery of the United States*, p. 28. Also, "American Pottery," *Buffalo Express* (21 April 1901).

71.   Folk potters of the period usually purchased their mineral pigments from commercial suppliers, and Ohr could certainly have done as much in New Orleans. His children remembered seeing him filing various metals into dust to be added to the raw glaze. Moreover we do know that at some time he used colorants supplied by "J. Marsching Co., 27 Park Place, New York, Importers of Mineral Colors, and Material for China and Glass Decoration." This firm had a full-page ad in the back of Susan Frackelton's book *Tried by Fire,* (New York: D. Appleton and Company, 1886).

72.   Documents from the National Museum of American History provided by R. L. Blaszczyk.

73.   "National Arts Club," *Keramic Studio* (February 1900): p. 212. Probably written by the editor, Adelaide Alsop Robineau.

74.   Jody Blake, "The Fair Years for Newcomb Pottery," unpublished master's thesis, Newcomb College (1983). It is possible that Ohr's trip to the Frackelton Pottery the year before might have had something to do with getting League sponsorship.

75.   *Times-Picayune.*

76.   Bensel, "Biloxi Pottery," p. 8.

77.   Ohr is mentioned briefly in Charles De Kay, "Art from the Kilns," *Munsey's Magazine* 26 (October 1901): p. 46.

78.   G. Slocum, "Club News," *Keramic Studio* (June 1901): p. 36. And from the private papers of R. Blasberg, courtesy of Faith Blasberg.

79.   W. King, "Ceramic Art at the Pan-American Exposition," *Crockery and Glass Journal* 53 (30 May 1901): p. 15. See also W. King, "Ceramic Art at the Pan-American Exposition," *Illustrated Glass and Pottery World* 9 (15 May 1901): p. 116.

80.   Blake, "Fair Years for Newcomb Pottery," p. 10.

81.   There are a number of articles describing ceramics at the exposition but none mentions Ohr. See, for example, "The National Arts Club Exhibit of Porcelain and Pottery at the Pan-American," *Keramic Studio* 3 (1901): p. 143; "National League Exhibit at the Pan-American," *Keramic Studio* 3 (1901): p. 173; "Arts and Crafts at the Pan-American," *New York Times,* 21 July 1901, p. 11; "Art Court at Pan-American," *New York Times,* 31 March 1901, p. 20.

82.   Edwin A. Barber, *The Pottery and Porcelain of the United States* (New York: J and J Publishing, 1901), p. 498.

83.   Incidentally, Barber, who was curator of the Pennsylvania Museum, donated two of Ohr's vessels to the museum. On February 12, 1901, Barber sent a letter to John T. Morris, a supporter of the museum, that reads: "I beg to acknowledge yours of the 11th with return of the Biloxi potter's letter. I wrote him, and will advise you as soon as I receive his reply. If he does not come to terms, I would not bother with him any longer, but forward the entire lot of pieces to Providence as he directs." From the private papers of R. Blasberg, courtesy of Faith Blasberg. One can only guess that Morris was attempting to acquire some pots for the museum from George, who wished them sent instead to the Arts and Crafts show in Providence.

84.   "Biloxi Heard From," *Crockery and Glass Journal* 53 (13 June 1901): p. 29. Note that George states that he has "20 years ability" implying the start of his career as around 1881.

85.   "Mississippi Trace," *Studio Potter,* p. 82.

86.   William Percival Jervis, *The Encyclopedia of Ceramics* (New York: Blanchard, 1902).

87.   Binns, in a letter to a Grace T. Thomas, dated April 17, 1922, wrote: "A manual skill such as you describe may be much more of a curse than a blessing. Witness George Orr [sic] of Biloxi. He had or has if he is still alive a fatal facility on the wheel but he employed it to make rubbish and thus diminished the whole value of pottery of this kind." New York State College of Ceramics Library, Alfred University.

Paul Cox remembered his old teacher having a somewhat different opinion of Ohr (c. 1903): "Binns had a small bowl by Ohr. . .and told me that the bowl was the work of a genius." Cox letter March 4, 1967.

88.   Ohr is mentioned briefly in W. G. Bowdoin, "Some American Pottery Forms," *Art Exchange* (April 1903): p. 87.

89.   Isabel McDougall, "Some Recent Arts and Crafts Work," *House Beautiful* 14 (July 1903): p. 69.

90.   Ethel Hutson, "Quaint Biloxi Pottery," *Clay Worker* 44 (September 1905): p. 225.

91.   A number of small bisque jugs and pots exist incised *Expo clay 1904,* and script signed G. E. Ohr. George had a little portable gasoline kiln and probably made and fired such pieces at the fair.

92.   *Times-Picayune.*

93.   Ibid. As Cox put it, "Meyer told me that Ohr went to the several Fairs and sold little and had to get back as best he could. I found when I tried that folks did not buy much pottery and when Ohr was at it I would guess that Biloxi visitors enjoyed seeing him work but bought little or nothing. And that he was not so dumb when he boxed it up and let it ripen with age." Cox letter March 4, 1967.

94.   The original survives in the possession of an Ohr family member in Mississippi.

95.   Hutson, "Quaint Biloxi Pottery," p. 225.

96.   See *Keramic Studio* of 1905: January, p. 93; February, p. 216; March, p. 251; April, p. 268; May, p. 7. In fact, one can hardly tell from the mainstream literature of the day that Ohr was even at the fair. See, for example, Frederic A. Whiting, "The Arts and Crafts at the Louisiana Purchase Exposition," *International Studio* 23 (October 1904): p. 385. There is no mention of him in the *Official Catalogue of Exhibitors Universal Exposition St. Louis, U.S.A. 1904 Division of Exhibits Department B Art.* He is pictured near a portable kiln in *Clay Worker* 44 (September 1905): p. 227. There is no text, but the caption places Ohr at the St. Louis Exposition even though the scene is the backyard of an armory. S. Geijsbeek, *Transactions of the American Ceramic Society* 7 (1905): p. 347, wrote (under the listing for Mississippi): "The greater part of the state exhibit in the Mines building was devoted to the products of the clay artist, George E. Ohr, of Biloxi,

articles in nearly all imaginable forms and designs. They were finished mostly in bright colored glazes, though some lustre and matt effects were found on several pieces."

97. "Annual Convention of United States Potters' Association," *Crockery and Glass Journal* 60 (December 1905): p. 217.

98. The records of the Smithsonian indicate that the selection was made from a group of eight pieces, not four.

99. *Times-Picayune.*

100. From private conversations with Dolores Davidson Smith. It's not known to what event this Boston Exposition actually referred. It is only remotely possible that it was the special tenth anniversary show put on by the Boston Arts and Crafts Society (1907). Ohr's name, however, does not appear in any of the literature describing the proceedings. See, for example, Eva Lovett, "The Exhibition of the Society of Arts and Crafts, Boston," *International Studio* 31 (March 1907): p. 27; Annie M. Jones, "Arts and Crafts Department," *Scrip* 2 (April 1907): p. 223. In Dolores Smith, "Echoes from the Past: George Ohr's Pottery," *Popular Ceramics* (September 1965): p. 8, the author writes, "Ohr exhibited his wares in the New Orleans Cotton Exposition, the St. Louis Exposition, the Jamestown Exposition, the Boston Exposition, the Atlanta Exposition, and other fairs, winning medals and blue ribbons wherever his work appeared." How accurate that statement is in all its particulars remains to be established, but at one time (the early 1970s) there was a plaque mounted with Ohr's medals and ribbons—it seems now to have disappeared somewhere in Biloxi.

101. "George Ohr visited the Jamestown Exposition and had to journey back by the equivalent of hitchhiking." So reported Cox, "Potteries of the Gulf Coast," p. 110. Dolores Smith makes the same claim in "Second Showing of the Pottery of George E. Ohr," p. 9. Nonetheless Ohr is not mentioned in Marcus Benjamin, "American Pottery at the Jamestown Exposition," *Glass and Pottery World* 15 (October 1907): p. 23. Nor is George listed anywhere in the *Official Blue Book of the Jamestown Ter-Centennial Exposition* (Norfolk, Va.: Colonial Publishing Company, 1909)—neither as an award winner, an exhibitor, nor as a concessionaire (which is the more likely). Still, he certainly could have been there. Incidentally, Benjamin was well aware of Ohr's work and had said some nice things

about it in his series of articles, "American Art Pottery," published in *Glass and Pottery World* (April 1907): p. 36. An Ohr vase from the Marcus Benjamin Collection was given to the Smithsonian in 1938.

102. A bisque vase has scrawled upon it very nearly the same "Mary had a little lamb" poem and is dated March 1, 1902. A small glazed plate is incised *Clo Ohr 1902*. A tall bisque vase bears the inscription *Made in the presence of owner John Power Biloxi 1–24–1903*. There are many bisque vases and bowls dated 1906 and several dated 1907. One reads: *Clay from JAB. Brick Clay 07* and a plaque is marked *7–3–07*. Another piece bears the cryptic inscription *Biloxi USA Jan 1st 10 AM 1907 $ SCAT.*

103. The use of the word *It* as a synonym for sex appeal was given its greatest popularity by the novelist Elinor Glyn (1927), although Kipling used it in the same sense earlier (1904). Madame Glyn found *it* in the silent movie star Clara Bow, whose meteoric career ended when the arrival of the talkies revealed her thick Brooklyn accent. What exactly George had in mind by calling himself the IT-Pot R, can only be imagined.

104. It should be pointed out that there was a long tradition of producing unglazed artware in this country and Ohr's fascination with it was not something extraordinary. Among others making unglazed vessels were the Chelsea Keramic Art Works (1868), Chicago Terra Cotta Works (1876), Halm Art Pottery (1877), Alexander Robertson at Roblin Art Pottery (1898), and later Charles Hyten at Niloak Pottery (1909). Ohr often used scroddling to produce a decorative, veined effect. Years before, when he occasionally made such pieces, he coated them with a clear glaze. After around 1900 he used the technique more frequently and apparently never glazed the work.

105. "The Potter of Biloxi," *Crockery and Glass Journal*, p. 49.

106. Most of the roughly ten thousand pieces of pottery were irreverently jumbled, crated, and neglected (having been tossed into open wooden boxes in 1910, without any packing material whatever), there to remain for forty-nine years. It was reported in 1922 (*Times-Picayune*) that several hundred vessels were on display and offered for sale in the family cottage. Though it is reasonable that George would have retained a number of pots rather than have them all stored in the garage, it's not known

when the practice of selling them from the home was initiated. The intention seems clear enough: "in a corner of the window frame is a small discolored sign: 'Pottery for sale.'" Beyond this apparent piecemeal public offering it was reported that "his widow wishes to sell the lot. She feels that she must. But she wishes to sell it all together. If some large concern would buy the lot, she would sell for $1 each." In 1935 Cox ("Potteries of the Gulf Coast," p. 110) wrote that Ohr's "sons still offer wares for sale . . . maintaining a sales room in their residence at Biloxi. They make little effort to sell, however, and the sign that hangs over the sidewalk on a side street must be looked for carefully to be observed." Since the machinery in the garage and the nearby railroad train often rattled the entire building, some of the pieces once stored in the attic show signs of decades of wear. Many entered the contemporary market in the 1970s still carrying thick patches of accumulated dust and grease; perhaps a quarter of them were damaged.

107. Cox first met Ohr in Biloxi, possibly in the summer of 1910, and they spent some time together along with Meyer. "I never saw the pottery pictured in *Popular Ceramics* [footnote 100]. I mean the building. When I met Ohr he had stopped making." Cox letter March 4, 1967. Since Cox visited with Ohr in his home next door to the former pottery building the implication is that it was already an automobile repair shop.

108. Meyer, Ohr, and Cox went up one of the rivers that emptied into Biloxi Bay to examine the clay deposit at Holly Bluff. "Well, the Sunday we made that trip to see Holly we started back to Biloxi so I [Cox] could get my train. I got it but when near the then rear of the town George decided we should stop and at a farm get a water melon. Meyer told Ohr truth which was that there were no melons but Ohr persisted and when the boat came near shore he took one of the heavy oars in in case of need [it was a motor-powered boat] and used it as a vaulting pole and broke half the blade off. He reported in time that there were no melons and then in the boat decided to adjust the engine which needed no such thing. The engine then would not run and so with five mile distance to cover Ohr took the oar with the good blade and handed me the lame one and Meyer steered and with me taking two to three strokes to one by Ohr we got to the Biloxi beach on which stood the Meyer home." Cox letter January 9, 1967.

109.   As Paul Cox related, "Now about meeting him when he was just out of jail. George Ohr I mean.

"Meyer was with me. We went to the Ohr cottage. Mrs. Ohr met us at the door and told Meyer whom she called Uncle Joe as did most of his Biloxi friends, and she told us that George was asleep on a cot as he had been in jail for ranting on the streets about how he had been cheated by the purchaser of a lot. He had stunted for a few days so the cops locked him up to take him off the streets.

"Mrs. Ohr took us up to the room where George was in the cot asleep. It had a mosquito bar hanging from a frame that if on a four poster bed would be the tester but in this case it was the ceiling. She wakned [sic] Ohr and told him that Uncle Joe was there with Mr. Cox. He pulled himself erect on the cot from rear part to his long hair and he pushed the bar aside, slipped his feet into straw slippers, blinked at me and said after a bit 'You think you are smart.' I replied that I did not think I was too smart and waited. He said after a rather long pause 'did you ever read the poem I wrote about you?' I replied I knew nothing about any poem so he got from under the pillow a wallet fat with papers of all sorts and searched for the poem and then read it to me. It was doggerel of a kind a dog would be ashamed of. It went on about how Newcomb Pottery had taken on a college trained ceramics man and how impossible it would be for a college to teach a person what he and Meyer knew and like stuff winding up with the statement the College Man could have the job but never could he do for the production what George Ohr could do.

"He finished and put the paper back in the wallet and the wallet under the pillow and sat on the edge of the cot blinking his black eyes at me. Finally he said 'you think I am crazy don't you?' I told him that Meyer had told me about him and that I did not think he was crazy and with that he stopped his act and remarked 'I found long ago it paid me to act this way.' From that time on if we met we dealt with each other as any two pottery experts would deal. No more poetry, no more telling me I was too smart etc.

"I suppose I spent maybe about three half days later on at different time with him and Meyer and always Ohr with me was just a fellow with me of the same interests but of course his pranks never stopped." Cox letter January 27, 1967.

110.   "Ohr came to the Meyer place. Mrs. Meyer was a fat French woman tho born in Louisiana. Meyer and Ohr were agnostics and Mrs. Meyer was deeply dyed Roman Catholic. In the front yard of the Biloxi place the two men started in to poke Mrs. Meyer about her profound faith in the many saints and that was the time when the silent movies had produced 'Quo Vadis.' In case you were born too late to know that epic it dealt with the Nero times and to mind comes the one about the little girl taken to see it who outside the show place wept bitterly. Asked why she wept she replied that one poor lion did not get any Christians to eat.

"Mrs. Meyer blew her top suddenly and said to Ohr 'You old Quo Vadis, you!' Both men then laughed and subsided." Cox letter January 9, 1967.

111.   "Most of what I know about Ohr," recalled Cox, "I had from Meyer. I think I wrote of his stunt when he rode his motor cycle attired in night shirt, with a crown of euphorbia which is a growth natural to the area, and a cross with sign painted 'The Persecuted One' to follow the Mardi Gras parade from Back Bay to the town center yelling and screeching and with his cycle horn on full and cut out making a fire cracker racket.

"I used to be told that George was on rampage by Meyer but I was never on hand when he was making a show." Cox letter January 9, 1967.

112.   Paul Evans, "Jalan: Transitional Pottery of San Francisco," *Spinning Wheel* (April 1973), p. 24. Cox, "Potteries of the Gulf Coast," p. 197.

113.   From a typed letter by Ohr to C. L. Alexander postmarked April 1, 1915. Biloxi Library.

114.   Ibid.

115.   Ibid.

116.   Ohr did sell his artware and sometimes even gave it away: Barber, King, and Benjamin each had Biloxi vessels in their collections. It seems that Louis Comfort Tiffany also owned at least one piece of Ohr's pottery. A small cream pitcher that probably survived the Laurelton Hall fire was on display in "The Treasures of Tiffany" show at the Chicago Museum of Science and Industry (1982).

117.   It is often maintained that Ohr had no effect whatever on the subsequent development of American pottery—but such a blanket conclusion seems imprudent. What influence he did have will certainly be difficult to determine. It's reasonable to assume, however, that any artist who saw his work would have been moved in one way or another, and that must have happened to many. Be-cause of Ohr's virtuosity and the icono-clastic nature of his art, emulating him directly would have been very improbable at the time—there was no school of Ohr disciples. Writing about the Shear-water Pottery of Ocean Springs, Cox ("Potteries of the Gulf Coast," p. 198) suggests that "in the main, they have copied from the work and inspirations of George Ohr and Joseph Meyer." In "The Mad Potter of Biloxi," *House and Garden* (June 1987): p. 104, K. Kertess mentions a link with Ken Price via an instructor at Alfred University in the late fifties who was an Ohr enthusiast. Though surely not widely known in the mid-twentieth century, Ohr was at least referenced in J. Ramsay, *American Potters and Pottery* (Clinton, Mass.: Hale, Cushman and Flint, 1939), p. 236; Warren E. Cox, *The Book of Pottery and Porcelain* (New York: Crown Publishers, 1944), p. 1101; and C. Jordan Thorn, *Handbook of Old Pottery and Porcelain Marks* (New York: Tudor Publishing Company, 1947), p. 141. When Marion John Nelson praised Ohr in "Art Nouveau in American Ceramics," *Art Quarterly of the Detroit Institute of Arts* 26:4 (1963): p. 441, it was quite matter-of-fact, as if any knowledgeable person in the field would know the name. His article pictured twenty-three major Ohr pots (part of Figure 21).

118.   *Times-Picayune.*

119.   Oto Ohr in "Mississippi Trace," *Studio Potter,* p. 83.

120.   Ohr's obituary in the *Biloxi Daily Herald,* 8 April 1918: "Surviving relatives besides the widow are four sons and one daughter." George and Josephine (d. 3/17/30) had ten children: Ella (b. 6/21/87, d. 1887), Asa (b. 1/18/89, d. 1893), Leo (b. 9/20/90), Clo (b. 5/1/92), Lio (b. 7/26/93, d. 1914), Oto (b. 9/11/95), Flo (b. 12/11/98, d. 1900), Zio (b. 10/5/1900, d. 1904), Ojo (b. 1/25/03), and Geo (b. 8/8/06). That same obituary remarks that "Mr. Ohr's work has been the marvel of the thousands of persons who have either purchased of him, or who learned of his genius. Even celebrated men such a Elbert Hubbard became interested in the man and his work. As a matter of fact, it is probable that he will rank with some of the most celebrated men of all times whose genius lies in handcraft."

"No Two Alike": The Triumph of Individuality

1. Lyle Saxon, "Wonderful Craftsmanship Shown by Biloxi Potter," *New Orleans Times-Picayune,* 1 October 1922.

2. George E. Ohr, "Biloxi Heard From," *Crockery and Glass Journal* 53 (13 June 1901): p. 29.

3. George E. Ohr, "Some Facts in the History of a Unique Personality," *Crockery and Glass Journal* 54 (12 December 1901): p. 123.

4. Ibid., p. 124.

5. "The Potter of Biloxi," *Crockery and Glass Journal* 70 (23 December 1909): p. 50.

6. Ohr, "A Unique Personality," p. 124.

7. Ellen P. Denker, *The Kirkpatricks' Pottery at Anna, Illinois* (Urbana-Champaign, Ill.: Krannert Art Museum, University of Illinois, 1986). Refer to this catalog for an extended discussion of the Kirkpatricks' work.

8. Della Campbell McLeod, "Ohr Pottery...," *Memphis Commercial Appeal,* 27 June 1909. This interview was the basis for an article entitled "The Potter of Biloxi" (see note 5 above).

9. From a copy of a faded compilation of Ohr's sayings set in three columns of type, which was presented to the author by Bobbie Davidson Smith, a lifetime friend of the Ohr family from Ocean Springs, Mississippi.

10. J. W. Carpenter, who purchased the whole Ohr legacy, has indicated that a glass copy of the famous Peach Blow vase, along with Ohr's copy of it, came with the collection. Ohr was able to simulate the shape but not the color. Technically, it would have been impossible for him to create the high-fired, transmutation peach blow glaze with his low-fired kiln and materials.

11. Robert W. Blasberg in *The Unknown Ohr* (Milford, Pa.: Peaceable Press, 1986), p. 29, points out the existence of glass prototypes for two of Ohr's molds, and, he suggests, "the nagging possibility remains that Ohr might have engaged in just the slightest bit of industrial piracy where some of the molds are concerned." This has since been confirmed. I am indebted to Bruce Aldini of New York City for his careful observations in pointing out two ceramic prototypes from Staffordshire, England. On p. 31, the mold in the photograph, center left, as well as the one on p. 32, both appear to have been taken from a pitcher made by Samuel Alcock & Company, c. 1830–59. The mold in the photograph, center right, also on p. 31, appears to have been taken from a pitcher made by C. Meigh, c. 1856–58. Furthermore, the two female figures on this piece have each been molded separately and used out of context in a mold to produce the Ohr pitcher on p. 33, center right.

12. *Handbook for the Use of Visitors Examining Pottery and Porcelain in the Museum,* The Metropolitan Museum of Art (New York, 1875).

13. W. P. Jervis in *The Encyclopedia of Ceramics* (New York: Blanchard, 1902), p. 81, indicates that the term *cadogan* originated in England when copies were made "at the Swinton Factory from an Indian model furnished by the Hon. Mrs. Cadogan." (The illustration Jervis used appears to be an eighteenth-century Chinese form.) He goes on to explain the concept: "From a hole in the bottom a tube slightly spiral was made to pass up inside the vessel to within half an inch of the top, so that after filling, the pot being turned over into its proper position for table use. the tea was retained without chance of spilling."

14. "The Potter of Biloxi," p. 50.

15. J.R.A. LeVine, *Linthorpe Pottery* (England: Teeside Museum Publication, 1970), p. 4.

16. Owen Jones, *The Grammar of Ornament* (London, 1856). In this work, Jones proposes thirty-seven "General Principles in the Arrangement of Form and Colour, in Architecture and the Decorative Arts."

17. Alf Bøe, *From Gothic Revival to Functional Form* (New York: Da Capo Press, 1979), pp. 24–26. This work gives a thorough discussion of the various aspects of the English design reform movement.

18. Ohr's sayings from Smith.

19. Ohr, "A Unique Personality," p. 125.

20. "The Potter of Biloxi," p. 50.

21. Ohr's sayings from Smith.

22. For additional information on the development of the New Orleans Art Pottery see: Jessie Poesch, *Newcomb Pottery* (Exton, Pa: Schiffer Publishing, 1984), pp. 12–13; Suzanne Ormond and Mary E. Irvine, *Louisiana's Art Nouveau* (Gretna, La.: Pelican Publishing, 1976), pp. 11–14.

23. "Concerning the Biloxi Potteries," *China, Glass and Pottery Review* 4 (April 1899): p. 49. The author quotes a sign hanging in Ohr's pottery workshop: "Erected in 1888 burned out and rebuilt in 1894."

24. R. W. Blasberg, *George E. Ohr and His Biloxi Art Pottery* (Port Jervis, N.Y.: J. W. Carpenter, 1973), p. 9. The center photograph contains a sign at top that reads: "G. E. Ohr of Biloxi Miss! His challenge has been standing for 17 years to meet any potter creating shapes." This photograph was probably taken at the 1904 St. Louis World's Fair.

25. For an extended discussion see Lewis Mumford, *The Brown Decades* (1931; reprint: New York: Dover Publications, 1971). Unfortunately ceramics are not discussed.

26. Martin Eidelberg, "The Ceramic Art of William H. Grueby," *Connoisseur* 184 (September 1973): p. 47.

27. W. A. King, "The Palissy of Biloxi," *Buffalo Express,* 12 March 1899.

28. Anton Ehrenzweig, *The Hidden Order of Art* (Berkeley: University of California Press, 1971), p. 66.

29. "Concerning the Biloxi Potteries," p. 48.

30. "The Potter of Biloxi," p. 49.

31. "Concerning the Biloxi Potteries," p. 48.

32. Eidelberg, "The Ceramic Art of William H. Grueby," p. 49.

33. George E. Ohr, letter to Col. C. L. Alexander dated 31 March 1915, Biloxi Public Library.

34. "Concerning the Biloxi Potteries," p. 49.

35. "The Potter of Biloxi," p. 49.

36. One of the many people committed to elevating the status of the designer and the decorative arts was Christopher Dresser. In his *Principles of Decorative Design* (London: Cassell, Petter, & Galpin, n.d. [1873]), p. 15, he declared, "Ornamentation is in the highest sense of the word a Fine Art; there is no art more noble, none more exalted. It can cheer the sorrowing; it can soothe the troubled; it can enhance the joys of those who make merry; it can inculcate the doctrine of truth; it can refine, elevate, purify, and point onward and upward to heaven and to God. It is a fine art, for it embodies and expresses the feelings of the soul of man."

37. Malcom Haslam, *The Martin Brothers Potters* (London: Richard Dennis, 1978), p. 114.

38. Martin Eidelberg and William R. Johnston, "Japonisme and French Decorative Arts," in *Japonisme,* Gabriel P.

Weisberg, ed. (Rutland, Vt.: Charles E. Tuttle, 1975), pp. 141–55. For an extended discussion of Japanism in France, refer to this enlightening essay.

39. Saxon, "Wonderful Craftsmanship."

40. Stephan Tschudi Madsen, *Sources of Art Noveau,* trans. Ragnar Christopherson (New York: Da Capo Press, 1976), 184.

41. Ibid., p. 187.

42. Ibid.

43. Dresser, *Principles,* p. 17.

44. Ohr, "Biloxi Heard From," p. 29.

45. McLeod, "Ohr Pottery."

46. George Kubler, *The Shape of Time* (New Haven: Yale University, 1962), pp. 65, 68.

47. Blasberg, *George E. Ohr,* p. 4. The photograph of Ohr in his stockroom includes a placard with this proclamation in the lower portion of the picture.

Clay Prophet: A Present Day Appraisal

1. Ohr in William Percival Jervis, *The Encyclopedia of Ceramics* (New York: Blanchard, 1902), p. 420.

2. "Pottery Wizard Dies in Biloxi," *Biloxi Daily Herald,* 8 April 1918.

3. See Lyle Saxon, "Wonderful Craftsmanship Shown by Biloxi Potter," *Times Picayune,* 1 October 1922. This article gives a touching account of the attempt by Ohr's widow to sell his pots: "If some large concern would buy the lot, she would sell them for $1 each." But true to Ohr's wishes she was only prepared to sell the thousands of pots as a group. Saxon's article is a delight. She was one of the first writers to express an intuitive understanding of Ohr's pots and their unusual forms. In a particularly evocative passage she describes how she was lured into the Ohr cottage by a small, weathered sign, POTTERY FOR SALE, and how she discovered the pots themselves. "You find yourself in a room which is filled from end to end with pottery; it stands on shelves, upon the floor, in the window sills. Tables are covered with it, and, as you look through the door of the adjoining room, you see other pieces, pitchers, groups of luster ware, vases, jars, lamps jumbled together in confusion—a veritable museum of spheres globes and romboids as well as pieces of irregular shape which you cannot name."

Saxon ended her piece by speculating upon the ultimate fate of these pieces. "Will it be scattered, sold for a song? Will it disappear from the earth? And will our grandchildren . . .years from now, search the antique shops in quest of a cracked mug, offering fabulous prices for a piece of pottery signed by George Ohr?"

4. In 1972 even Ralph and Terry Kovel declared that "it is doubtful that many pieces of Ohr pottery exist outside of museums today." See "The Mad Potter of Biloxi," *Western Collector* 5 (May 1972): p.43.

5. From an interview with John Coplans, New York City, March 15, 1975. I am greatly indebted to Coplans for introducing me to Ohr's work in a manner that, from the outset, opened many doors to the prophecy and complexity of his pots. I had sought out Coplans after being given a copy of Blasberg's monograph on Ohr by the Funk ceramist Clayton Baily. I arrived just after the then-editor of *Craft Horizons* had left. Coplans was chuckling about the fact that he and Rose Slivka had had a heated argument over the pots with Slivka insisting that the pots were simply too thin and too delicate, and that "they could simply not be thrown by hand."

In his living room I handled my first Ohr pots, carefully taken down from a high shelf. They were not major works but they were nonetheless mesmerizing, passionate little objects. By the time I left his apartment, my obsession with Ohr's pots had begun to take root.

Coplans had developed a formidable reputation as a freewheeling critic with *Artforum*. He was an authority on painters Roy Lichtenstein and Andy Warhol and had written about developments in contemporary American ceramic art as well. He was the first critic from the fine arts to champion the work of Peter Voulkos and his students. In 1966 he organized the exhibition *Abstract Expressionist Ceramics* for the Art Gallery, Univerity of California at Irvine, a pivotal show in announcing the arrival of a revolutionary aesthetic in American ceramics. He was, as a result, uniquely qualified to see Ohr both from the specialized world of ceramics and in the broader context of the arts. His early enthusiasm for Ohr was infectious and he encouraged many in the New York art world to collect Ohr's pots. Soon after our meeting he sold his collection to finance his new love, photography.

6. George Kubler, *The Shape of Time* (New Haven, Conn.: Yale University Press, 1962), p. 33. Kubler explains that:

Every important work of art can be regarded both as a historical event and as a hard-won solution to some problem. It is irrelevant now whether the event was original or conventional, accidental or willed, awkward or skillful. The important clue is that any solution points to the existence of some problem to which there have been other solutions, and that other solutions to this same problem will most likely be invented to follow the one now in view. As the solutions accumulate, the problem alters. The chain of solutions nevertheless discloses the problem.

As Kubler points out, "The outstanding innovator amongst artists, like Caravaggio, is functionally lonely. His break with tradition may or may not be known to the multitude, but he is himself of necessity aware of the isolation it brings. . . .Usually the entire range and bearing of such a career can only be brought into focus after death, when we can place it in relation to preceding and subsequent events."

7. George E. Ohr, "Some Facts in the History of a Unique Personality," *Crockery and Glass Journal* 54 (December 1901): p. 123.

8. Ohr in Paul Evans, "Reflections of Frederick Hurten Rhead," *Pottery Collectors Newsletter* 9 (September/October 1980): p. 45. This criticism of Ohr's originality was particularly amusing coming from Rhead, who was a plagiarist *par excellence.* All his designs for industry are loosely based on well-known wares of his day. Even the "Fiesta" ware designs for Homer Laughlin, for which he became famous in the 1930s, were simply cleaned up versions of the brightly colored "California monochromes" that were in production a decade before "Fiesta" made its appearance. But originality of form was not a priorty for the pottery movement in the United States. A far greater value was placed upon style and "good taste."

9. Ohr in Della Campbell McLeod, "Ohr Pottery. . . ," *Commercial Appeal,* 27 June 1909.

10. Ibid.

11. In Jer. 18:1–6 in the King James version of the Bible, there is another passage that deals with the theme of the "marred" pot:

Arise and go down to the potter's house, and there I will cause thee to hear my words. Then I went down to the potter's house, and, behold, he wrought a work on the wheels. And the vessel that he made of clay was marred in the hand of the potter, so he made it again another vessel, as seemed good to the potter to make it. The word of the Lord came to me, saying, O house of Israel, cannot I do with you as this potter? saith the Lord. Behold, as the clay is in the potter's hand, so are ye in mine hand, O house of Israel.

12. Ohr in McLeod, "Ohr Pottery. . ." Ohr showed particular affection towards his marred and killed babies. This could have been a sentimental reaction to the loss of several of his own children early in their lives. William King notes that if a visitor to Ohr's pottery showed particular sensitivity to his work, Ohr would "as a great concession" entrust them with the custody of one of these fire-damaged pots as a gesture of affection and trust. One of Ohr's earliest and most enthusiastic supporters, King was himself given such a piece. It could also be that the canny Ohr used these pieces to distract the more serious visitors from purchasing his art pots, which for all his commercial promotion he seemed most reluctant to sell.

13. See Peter Selz, *Funk Art* (Berkeley, Ca.: University Art Museum, University of California at Berkeley, 1967). This exhibition catalogue and the accompanying essay explain the Funk spirit, if not the style. See also chapter 9 in Garth Clark, *American Ceramics: 1876 to the Present* (New York: Abbeville Press, 1988).

14. "Concerning the Biloxi Potteries," *China, Glass and Pottery Review* 4 (April 1899): p. 47.

15. Ohr in McLeod, "Ohr Pottery. . ."

16. Later I had this instinctive association reinforced by a major Dada collector known by the pseudonym of Jedermann N.A., who has in the past few years become a collector of Ohr's pots. Jedermann had collected Duchamp's readymades from his Wedge of Chastity series and was first drawn to Ohr's pots by what he felt was a corresponding sensibility between the readymades and the sexual symbolism and wit in Ohr's pots.

17. Ohr, *"A Unique Personality,"* p. 123. This refers to the fable (somewhat distorted) of the ugly duckling. It was Ohr's way of identifying himself as a maverick, and potentially a swan.

18. Ohr in McLoed, "Ohr Pottery. . ."

19. The letter is reproduced in full in William King, "Ceramic Art at the Pan-American Exposition." *Crockery and Glass Journal* 53 (30 May 1901): p. 287. Ohr's claim was put to the test by the editor of *Brick* magazine who visited the potter in 1899. In "A Biloxi Pottery" (*Brick*, July 1987) he verified the following demonstration of Ohr's talent: "'Won't you show us how you

work,' we asked, and tying on a long apron he seized a lump of clay and keeping time to a Southern song as he worked, soon placed it upon the wheel. First a flower pot, then a jar with a cob stopper made of clay: form after form was brought out in rapid succession until finally it assumed the graceful outlines of a Greek urn, and after the potter and the editor had inscribed their names and the date upon the side, it was set away to be burned and shipped to Chicago."

20. Ohr in McLeod, "Ohr Pottery. . ."

21. Interview with the author, February 14, 1980, at the Dome, Oakland, California.

22. For a detailed account of the energies and innovations of Voulkos and the Otis group, see chapter 8 in Garth Clark, *American Ceramics: 1978 to the Present* (New York: Abbeville Press, 1987). See also Rose Slivka, *Peter Voulkos: A Dialogue with Clay* (Boston: New York Graphic Society, 1978).

23. See Rose Slivka, "The New Ceramic Presence," *Craft Horizons* 21 (July/August 1961).

24. Hamada in Bernard Leach, *A Potter's Book* (London: Faber and Faber, 1940), p. 40.

25. For a detailed account of the difference in style and circumstances between Ohr and Robineau, see "Ohr/Robineau: A Study in Polarities," *Transactions of the Ceramics Symposium 1979* (Los Angeles: Institute for Ceramic History, 1980): pp. 15–22.

26. Ethel Hutson, "Quaint Biloxi Pottery," *Clay Worker* 44 (September 1905): p. 3.

27. Oto Ohr in *Studio Potter* 10:2 (1981–82): p. 82.

28. Jean Cocteau quoted in Daniel Henry Kahnweiler, *Pablo Picasso — Ceramic* (Hanover, Germany: 1958), p. 6.

29. Jeff Perrone, "Entrées: Diaretics: Entreaties: Bowing (Wowing) Out," *Arts Magazine* 59 (April 1985).

30. Marion John Nelson, "Art Nouveau in American Ceramics," *Art Quarterly* 26, no. 4 (1963): p. 443.

31. Edwin Atlee Barber, *The Pottery and Porcelain of the United States* (New York: G. P. Putnam, 1901), p. 498.

32. William A. King, "Biloxi Pottery," *Buffalo Express,* 21 April 1900.

33. "High Art at Biloxi, Miss.," *New York Sun,* 22 December 1898.

34. Arturo Schwarz, *The Complete Works of Marcel Duchamp* (New York: Abrams, 1969). p. 79.

35. Ibid. p. 80.

36. Jervis, *The Encyclopedia of Ceramics,* p 420.

37. Quoted in Robert W. Blasberg's *George E. Ohr and His Biloxi Pottery* (Port Jervis, N.Y.: J. W. Carpenter, 1973).

38. Hutson, "Quaint Biloxi Pottery," p. 3.

39. "Biloxi Pottery from an Artistic Standpoint," *China, Glass and Pottery Review* 4 (June 1899): p. 21. The writer went on to remark that Ohr's antics suggested the circus sideshow, "the ravings of the Midway tooter and the advance agent of the minstrel troupe."

40. Evans, "Reflections."

41. See Samuel Robineau, "Adelaide Alsop Robineau," *Design* (April 1929): pp. 202–23, for a discussion of Robineau's marketing problems.

42. Hutson, "Quaint Biloxi Pottery," p. 3.

43. In the spring of 1983 I was invited by Peter Fusco (then the curator of decorative arts at the Los Angeles County Museum of Art) to inspect some recent ceramic acquisitions. Fusco had just acquired a small but handsome pot by Ohr and five works by Bernard Palissy. When I turned Palissy's pots over I was surprised to find that the undersides were startlingly close to the surfaces of Ohr's pot. Palissy had dappled the undersides with a polychrome mix of colors.

It is the considered opinion of my colleagues that this closeness in glaze treatment is purely accidental, as it was most unlikely that Ohr could have had access to Palissy's pottery. Certainly there were no collections of Palissy known in the New Orleans area at the time that Ohr was actively potting, nor any records of exhibitions of the French mannerist's work.

However, I am not as sure as my colleagues that Ohr did not see and have access to works in the *style* of Palissy. Ohr does say that he wishes to give to ceramics in form what Palissy gave to the medium in color. This implies a knowledge and understanding of Palissy's palette. In addition, other potters were inspired by Palissy in the late nineteenth century. For instance, Ellen P. Denker records in the catalogue *The Kirkpatricks' Pottery at Anna, Illinois* (Urbana-Champaign, Ill.: Krannert Art Museum, University of Illinois, 1986) that these country potters appear to have been influenced by Palissy. The extent to which Ohr was directly influenced by Palissy in his glazing technique must remain a matter of speculation for the moment until more convincing evidence can be obtained.

44. The term *Palissystes* is used to refer to those potters in France who took part in a revival of Palissy-ware during the mid-nineteenth century. This was the beginning of what was incorrectly known as "artistic faience," actually a low-fired art pottery. The revival of these wares began what was to grow into a major studio-pottery movement in France. Charles-Jean Avisseau (1796–1861) was one of the most prominent and influential figures amongst the *Palissystes,* influencing other potters including Leom Brard (1830–1902) and George Pull (1810–89). For a while the Palissy-ware was all the rage and widely exhibited. Possibly Ohr could have had access to works by these potters and to some of the commercially produced imitations of their work.

45. John Perreault, "Either Ohr," *Village Voice* (5 March 1985).

46. Octavio Paz, *The Castle of Purity.* Also see Carlo McCormick, "Exits and Entrances," *Artforum* 26 (January 1988), pp. 4–7, for a discussion of the clown in art. McCormick sees the role of clown as the "humanization of a warped character."

47. The first exhibition of Ohr's work since 1906 took place in 1966. Organized by Dolores "Bobby" Davidson Smith, it was an inauspicious return to the exhibition circuit. Smith, a friend of the Ohr family and dedicated promoter of Ohr, organized a showing of Ohr's pots at the Gulf South Ceramic Show, October 8 to 10, 1966. The show took place at the Bridgewater Mall on Highway 90 between Gulfport and Biloxi. See Dolores Smith, "Echoes from the Past: George Ohr's Pottery," *Popular Ceramics* (September 1965): pp. 8–11.

The next exhibition was organized by Patti Carr Black at the Mississippi State Historical Museum in Jackson from April 21 to May 31, 1978. A small catalogue was published with an essay by the author. This was followed in 1983 by a small traveling exhibition, *George E. Ohr: The Mad Biloxi Potter,* comprising thirty-two modest pieces and a catalogue. The show was arranged by Ron Dale at the University of Mississippi. Among other venues, the exhibition was shown at the High Museum in Atlanta.

In 1984 I organized a loan exhibition at my New York gallery entitled *George E. Ohr: An Artworld Homage.* The works came from painter Jasper Johns, arts attorney Carl Lobell, Dada collector Jedermann N.A., and contemporary art dealers Miani Johnson, Irving Blum, and Charles Cowles. This was the first individual exhibition of Ohr's pottery in New York City and it attracted considerable interest from the press.

Ohr has been seen mainly in group exhibitions such as Princeton University's *The Arts and Crafts Movement in America, 1876–1916* (1972), the Everson Museum's traveling survey, *A Century of Ceramics in the United States 1878–1978* (1979), the Ceramics Art Society's *From Our Native Clay* (1987), and other surveys.

48. John Russell, "Art: Jasper Johns Show Is Painting at Its Best," *New York Times* (3 February 1984).

49. Perrone, "Entrees."

50. John Perreault, "Either Ohr," *Village Voice* (5 March 1985).

Anderson, Alexandra. "George Ohr's 'Mud Babies.'" *Art in America* 67 (January–February 1979).

"Annual Convention of the United States Potters' Association." *Crockery and Glass Journal* 60 (December 1905).

"Arts and Crafts at the Pan American." *New York Times,* 31 March 1901.

Barber, Edwin Atlee. *Marks of American Potters.* Philadelphia: Patterson and White, 1904.

———. *The Pottery and Porcelain of the United States.* New York: G. P. Putnam's Sons, 1902.

Benjamin, Marcus. *American Art Pottery.* Washington, D.C., 1907. Originally published in *Glass and Pottery World* 15 (February–May 1907).

Bensel, L. M. "Biloxi Pottery." *Art Interchange* 46 (January 1901).

"Biloxi Heard From." *Crockery and Glass Journal* 53 (June 1901).

"A Biloxi Pottery." *Brick* (July 1897).

"Biloxi Pottery from an Artistic Standpoint." *China, Glass and Pottery Review* 4 (June 1899).

Blake, Jody. "The Fair Years for Newcomb Pottery." Master's thesis, Newcomb College, 1983.

Blasberg, Robert W. *George E. Ohr and His Biloxi Art Pottery.* Port Jervis, N.Y.: J. W. Carpenter, 1972.

———. *The Unknown Ohr: A Sequel to the 1973 Monograph.* Milford, Pa.: Peaceable Press, 1986.

Bowdoin, W. G. "Some American Pottery Forms." *Art Interchange* 50 (April 1903).

Carpenter, J. W. "Geo. Ohr's 'Pot-Ohr-E.'" *Antique Trader Weekly,* 19 September 1972.

Clark, Garth. *American Ceramics, 1876 to the Present.* New York: Abbeville Press, 1988.

———. "Avant Garde Volumes." *Studio Potter* 12 (December 1983).

———. *The Biloxi Art Pottery of George E. Ohr.* Jackson, Miss.: State Historical Museum, 1978.

———. *A Century of Ceramics in the United States, 1878–1978.* New York: E. P. Dutton, 1979.

———. "George E. Ohr." *Antiques* 128 (September 1985).

———. "George Ohr: Clay Prophet." *Craft Horizons* 38 (October 1978).

———. "Ohr/Robineau: A Study in Polarities." In *Transactions of the Ceramics Symposium, 1979.* Los Angeles: Institute for Ceramic History, 1980

———. "When I found the Potter's Wheel, I felt it all over like a Wild Duck in Water." *American Ceramics* 4 (1985).

"Concerning the Biloxi Potteries." *China, Glass and Pottery Review* 4 (April 1899).

Cox, Paul E. "Newcomb Pottery Active in New Orleans." *American Ceramic Society Bulletin* 22 (1933).

———. "Potteries of the Gulf Coast: An Individualistic Ceramic Art District." *Ceramic Age* 25 (April 1935).

Cummins, V. R. *Rookwood Pottery Potpourri.* Silver Springs, Md.: Cliff R. Leonard and Duke Coleman, 1980.

DeKay, Charles. "Art from the Kilns." *Munsey Magazine* 24 (October 1901).

Dietz, Ulysses. *The Newark Museum Collection of American Art Pottery.* Newark, N.J.: Newark Museum, 1984.

Earle, Mary Tracy. *The Wonderful Wheel.* New York: Century Co., 1896.

Eidelberg, Martin. "Art Pottery." In Robert Judson Clark, ed., *The Arts and Crafts Movement in America, 1876–1916.* Princeton, N.J.: Princeton University, 1972.

Ellison, Robert A., Jr. In Martin Eidelberg, ed., *From Our Native Clay: Art Pottery from the Collections of The American Ceramic Arts Society.* New York: Turn of the Century Editions, 1987.

Evans, Paul F. *Art Pottery of the United States: An Encyclopedia of Producers and Their Marks.* New York: Charles Scribner's Sons, 1974.

———. "Reflections of Frederick Hurten Rhead." *Pottery Collectors Newsletter* 9 (September–October 1980).

Febres, George. "The Mad Potter of Biloxi: To Be Ohr Not To Be." New Orleans Museum of Art *Arts Quarterly* 3 (October–December 1981).

Geijsbeek, S. "The Ceramics of the Louisiana Purchase Exhibition." *American Ceramic Society Transactions* 7 (1905).

Grootkerk, Paul. "George Ohr: The Biloxi 'Orh-na-ment.'" *Southern Quarterly,* Fall–Winter 1985.

Hecht, Eugene. "An Ohr Primer: Part I—The Grand Deceit." *American Art Pottery* 67 (December 1981).

———. "An Ohr Primer: Part II—A Chronology with Beasties." *American Art Pottery* 73 (June 1982).

———. "An Ohr Primer: Part III—The Artist and the Bad Guys." *American Art Pottery* 93 (February 1984).

———. "An Ohr Primer: Part IV—Ohr Deal by Fire." *American Art Pottery* 97 (June 1984).

———. "Gustav and Quixote." *American Art Pottery* 67 (December 1981).

———. "Mr. Pig and the Caterpillars." *American Art Pottery* 69 (February 1982).

———. "Newcomb Pottery: An Enterprise for Southern Women." *Antiques and the Arts Weekly* 1 (June 1985).

Heissenbuttel, Orva. "The Biloxi Art Pottery of George E. Ohr." *American Art Pottery* 5 (October 1976).

Hutson, Ethel. "Quaint Biloxi Pottery." *Clay Worker* 44 (September 1905).

Jervis, William P. *The Encyclopedia of Ceramics.* New York: Blanchard, 1902.

Jones, Annie M., "Arts and Crafts Department." *Scrip* 2 (April 1907).

Kahn, Barry. "A Century of Ceramics." *Monthly Detroit,* September 1981.

Keen, Kirsten Hoving. *American Art Pottery, 1875–1930.* Wilmington Del.: Delaware Art Museum, 1978.

Kertess, Klaus. "The Mad Potter of Biloxi." *House and Garden* 159 (June 1987).

King, William A. "Ceramic Art at the Pan American Exposition." *Crockery and Glass Journal* 53 (30 May 1901).

———. "The Palissy of Biloxi." *Buffalo Express,* 12 March 1899.

———. "Biloxi Pottery." *Buffalo Express,* 21 April 1900.

Kovel, Ralph, and Terry Kovel. *The Kovels' Collectors Guide to American Art Pottery.* New York: Crown, 1974.

———. "The Mad Potter of Biloxi." *Western Collector* 5 (May 1972).

Lieby, Joyce M. "George Ohr—The Potter's Potter." *Antique Collecting* 1 (August 1977).

Loring, John. "American Art Pottery." *Connoisseur* 200 (April 1979).

McDougall, Isabel. "Some Recent Arts and Crafts Work." *House Beautiful* 14 (July 1903).

McLeod, Della Campbell. "Ohr Pottery . . ." *Memphis Commercial Appeal,* 27 June 1909.

"Monsieur Gabry's Wheel." *Brick,* May 1898.

Nelson, Marion John. "Art Nouveau in American Ceramics." *Art Quarterly* 26, no. 4 (1963).

Ohr, George E. "Some Facts in the History of a Unique Personality." *Crockery and Glass Journal* 54 (December 1901).

Ohr, Oto. "Mississippi Trace: Interview—Oto Ohr." *Studio Potter* 10, no. 2 (1981–82).

Ormond, Suzanne, and Mary E. Irvine. *Louisiana's Art Nouveau: The Crafts of the Newcomb Style.* Gretna, La.: Pelican Publishing, 1976.

Perreault, John. "Either Ohr." *Village Voice,* 5 March 1985.

Perrone, Jeff. "Entrées: Diaretics: Entreaties: Bowing (Wowing) Out." *Arts Magazine* 59 (April 1985).

Poesch, Jessie. *Newcomb Pottery.* Exton, Pa.: Schiffer Publishing, 1984.

"The Potter of Biloxi." *Crockery and Glass Journal* 70 (23 December 1909).
"Pottery Wizard Dies in Biloxi." *Biloxi Daily Herald,* 8 April 1918.
Ralph, J. "The Sunny Mississippi." *Harper's New Monthly Magazine* 90 (May 1895).
Ramsay, John. *American Potters and*

Pottery. Boston: Hale, Cushman & Flint, 1939.
Reif, Rita. "Rediscovering a Potter." *New York Times,* 24 February 1985.
Saxon, Lyle. "Wonderful Craftsmanship Shown by Biloxi Pottery." *New Orleans Times-Picayune,* 1 October 1922.
Smith, Dolores. "Echoes from the Past:

George Ohr's Pottery." *Popular Ceramics* 17, no. 2 (September 1965).
Thorn, C. Jordan. *Handbook of Old Pottery and Porcelain Marks.* New York: Tudor Publishing, 1947.
Wiltshire, W. E. *Folk Pottery of the Shenandoah Valley.* New York: E. P. Dutton, 1975.

Index

Page numbers in *italics* refer to illustrations.

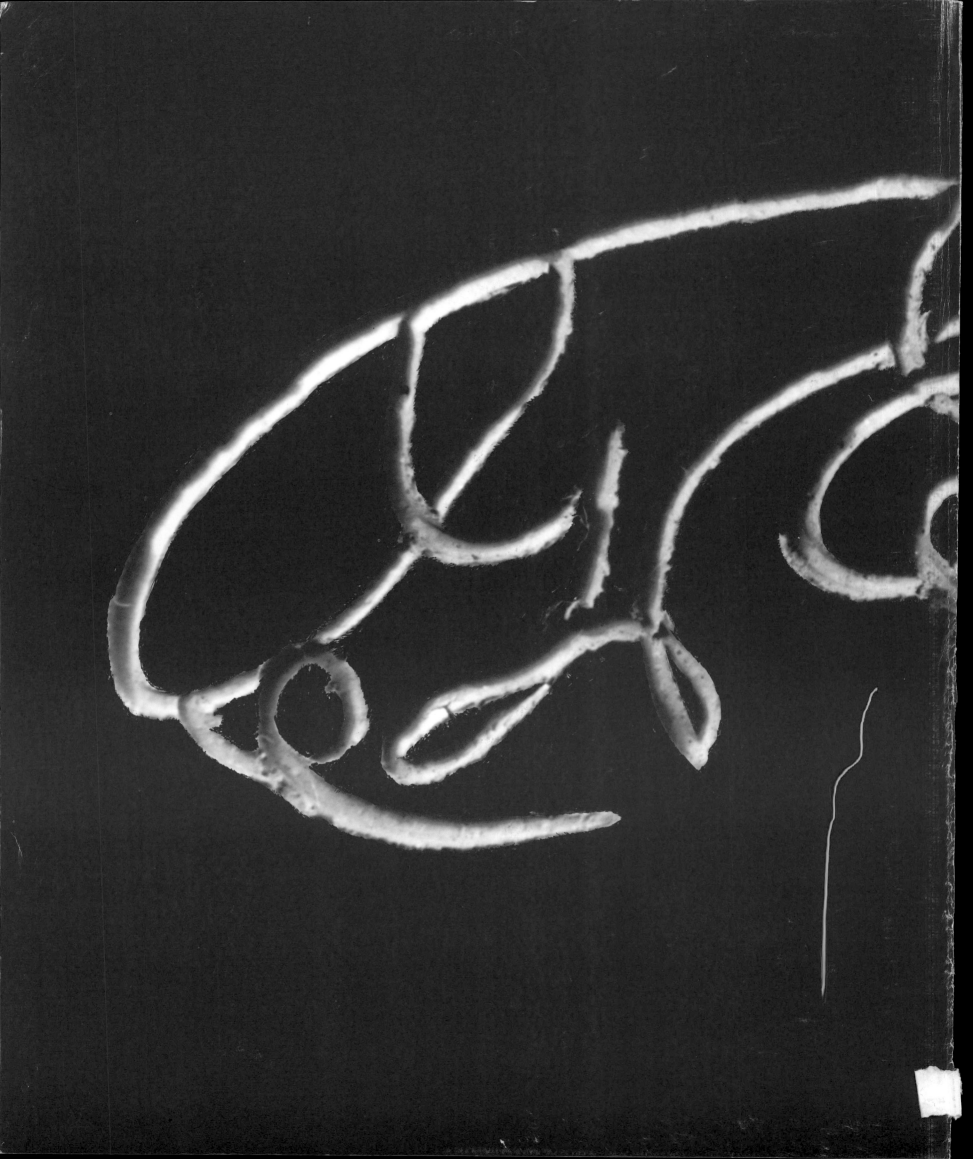